A New Owner's
Guide to
DACHSHUNDS

JG-110

Opposite page: Ch. Boondox Chaps, a standard Longhair owned by Dr. Roger and Debbie Brum and Sherry Snyder.

The Publisher wishes to acknowledge the following owners of the dogs in this book: Judy Anderson, Diana Bartlett, Liz A. Bernel, Georjan Bridger, Dr. Roger and Debbie Brum, Monica Canestrini, Anne Carson, Catherine Carson, Lynn Cope, Fred DelVecchio, Ed Docke, Andree Duchateau, Pam Fleming, Polly Fleming, Margaret Florenzano, Juan Rabasseda Gasçon, Lorraine Genieczko, Dan and Megan Hicks, Candy and Carl Holder, Helen and Neal Hamilton, Helen Hollingsworth, Harvey and Tracy Kratzer, Kaye Ladd, Jane K. Larsen, Gina Leone, Patricia Leone, Robert Leipheimer, Iris Love, Col. Katharine E. Manchester, Mary Jean Martin, Cathy Marzluf, Sue McClelland, John Merriman, Patti Nelson, Sandy Patterson, Barbara L. Powers, Margaret Pruitt, Sally Rubin, Sandy Russell, Denise Siemessen, Sherry Snyder, Sidney Stafford, Tamee Starnes, Bill Tack, Ruth Teeter, Anne Watkins, Gwen Wexler, Ann and Bob Wlodkowski.

Photographers: S. Abernathy Photography, Paulette Braun, Tara Darling, Isabelle Francais, Guy Kullander, Kaye Ladd, Gina Leone, Robert Pearcy, Vince Serbin, Robert Smith, Sidney Stafford, Chuck Tatham, Orin Paul Trademan Photography, Anne Watkins.

The author acknowledges the contribution of Judy Iby of the following chapters: Sport of Purebred Dogs, Identification and Finding the Lost Dog, Traveling with Your Dog, Health Care, Behavior and Canine Communication.

Distributed in the UNITED STATES to the Pet Trade by T.F.H. Publications, Inc., One T.F.H. Plaza, Neptune City, NJ 07753; distributed in the UNITED STATES to the Bookstore and Library Trade by National Book Network, Inc. 4720 Boston Way, Lanham MD 20706; in CANADA to the Pet Trade by H & L Pet Supplies Inc., 27 Kingston Crescent, Kitchener, Ontario N2B 2T6; Rolf C. Hagen Inc., 3225 Sartelon St. Laurent-Montreal Quebec H4R 1E8; in CANADA to the Book Trade by Vanwell Publishing Ltd., 1 Northrup Crescent, St. Catharines, Ontario L2M 6P5 ; in ENGLAND by T.F.H. Publications, PO Box 15, Waterlooville PO7 6BQ; in AUSTRALIA AND THE SOUTH PACIFIC by T.F.H. (Australia), Pty. Ltd., Box 149, Brookvale 2100 N.S.W., Australia; in NEW ZEALAND by Brooklands Aquarium Ltd. 5 McGiven Drive, New Plymouth, RD1 New Zealand; in Japan by T.F.H. Publications, Japan—Jiro Tsuda, 10-12-3 Ohjidai, Sakura, Chiba 285, Japan; in SOUTH AFRICA by Lopis (Pty) Ltd., P.O. Box 39127, Booysens, 2016, Johannesburg, South Africa. Published by T.F.H. Publications, Inc.
MANUFACTURED IN THE
UNITED STATES OF AMERICA
BY T.F.H. PUBLICATIONS, INC.

A NEW OWNER'S GUIDE TO DACHSHUNDS

KAYE LADD

Contents

Dachshunds will do just about anything for attention!

Longhaired Dachshunds have elegant, flowing coats.

Cuddle up with a Dachshund.

A big Dachshund kiss for a little friend.

A trio of roughhousing Smooth pups.

HISTORY of the Dachshund

Dachshund history is a special blend of fact, theory, and fiction. Every lover of the breed puts it together his own way. With the information available, there are unlimited versions. Many believe the Dachshund has been in existence for 4000 years. Ancient Egypt produced a portrayal of a dog on the monument of Thutmose III circa 1468 B.C. Although this doesn't look like a Dachshund, it does have a hieroglyphic type inscription that reads, "teka" or "tekar." Some believe this word is a root to the German word "Teckel" used to describe these long, low-bodied hounds. Others state that this word is probably more related to "teque," which translates to fiery.

Following the marriage of the Holy Roman Emperor Maximilan I to Marie of Burgundy in 1477, John Hutchinson Cook, one of the great historians of our breed, believed that the noble little Dachshund descended from the Burgundian hounds brought to Austria by the Hapsburgs. History documents long-bodied, low dogs referred to as teckels, earthdogs, and badger dogs throughout the 1500s and 1600s. Clearly the Dachshund breed was firmly in development. It was used to hunt underground, or at least to pursue small game underground.

Woodcuts dating back to 1582 by Jost Ammons depict the Dachshund with a docked tail. In 1671, a German book on hunting and falconry discusses a little dog that was used for tracking rabbits and that had crooked or straight legs and was feisty enough to chase badgers or foxes. Another book published in 1700 speaks of the ancestors of today's Dachshunds. In a section on "Badger, Otter and Beaverdogs," the author states, "These three varieties have about the same hunting accomplishments, but the first variety is especially suited to go after badgers. The French call these particular dogs Bassets, because of their low structure, long slender body and their low, somewhat turned in little legs." Some of these long dogs looked like smooth and longhaired Dachshunds of today, but the characteristics were still quite diverse well into the 1700s.

Some were said to look more terrier-like and others to more closely resemble pinschers. Wherever or whatever they were, these earthdogs were primarily the property of the nobility and gentry of the time.

During these developing times, Dachshunds and Bassets probably claim many of the same ancestors. "Basset" simply meant low of the leg, close to the ground. One historic reference book states that the offspring were divided. The big, lower-eared ones were called Bassets and the small, snippier ones were called Dachshunds. Perhaps this was similar to what we see regularly in the French wirehaired Petit Basset Griffon Vendéen where there is both a petite and a grand version.

An early theory states that the Dachshund and the Basset evolved from the same ancestry—the larger dogs were called Bassets and the smaller dogs were called Dachshunds.

Though I own a lithograph from the early 1900s where Bassets and Dachshunds were still shown together at the same show in London, I do not believe that these two breeds were interbred past the early 1800s. However, believing that

they were interbred certainly explains the origin of our piebald Dachshunds which create so much interest in the show ring today.

As a paramount hunting dog bred for the purpose of tracking prey to their dens, Dachshunds gained popularity for both this trait and their friskiness. They were even used at wild boar shoots, as they could avoid the boar and get under the brush.

Queen Victoria is known for her love of her Dachshund. Her consort, Prince Albert of Saxe-Goethe, is credited with bringing the breed to her. She actually chastised one lord for accusing the dog of having crooked legs. She also loved to dress up dear sweet little "Dash" in a scarlet jacket and trousers. The minute Queen Victoria named her Dachshund, Dash, we knew she lacked certain creative powers, but she certainly adored the dog. She even penned several drawings of him, which are highly prized.

Since the involvement of Queen Victoria in the 1840s, Dachshunds have progressed rapidly to the wonderful breed we know today. If you look at pictures of Dachshunds in the early 1900s, the crooked legs and irregular toplines are readily seen. Today, these have been dramatically straightened and corrected.

In England, Dachshunds so advanced in popularity that their first Specialty show, combined with Bassets, was held in 1886. There were over 200 dogs entered.

In America, the Dachshund Club of America was born in 1895. It is the eighth oldest breed club member of the American Kennel Club. By 1914, Dachshunds were already in the top ten breeds exhibited at the Westminster Kennel Club Show.

World War I set the breed back for what seemed like an eternity. Anything German was scorned. Owners of these personable dogs

Adult and puppy longhaired Dachshunds show off one of the three Dachshund coat types. Longhairs made their conformation debut at the 1923 Crufts show.

Duchwood's Cornerstone MS is a miniature Smooth who made quite a splash in the show ring with her controversial, yet spectacular, piebald coloration.

were harassed. Even the German name "Dachshund" was changed to "badger dog" to make it sound less Germanic.

By the 1930s and 40s, Dachshunds were Dachshunds again. Even World War II couldn't daunt the popularity of this little dog. He was now as American as the hot dog.

Early American kennel names that highly influenced the breed include Badger Hill, Hanheim's, Marienlust, Heying-Teckel, Albion, Ketal, De sangpur, Dunkeldort, Gera, White Gables, Farmeadow, Barhar, Will-o-Mar, Rose Farm, Crosswynd, Bayard, Dychland, Caseway, Moffet's Timbar, and Barbadox.

More current names of contributing "artistic breeders" include Barkersville, Han-Jo's, Boondox, v Westphalen, Walmar, Sleepy Hollow, Siddachs, Bergmarg, Bristleknoll, Jeric's, E.J.'s, Villanol's, Braaehaus, Sleepytime, Karchaus, Whistlestop, Canterbury, Roushland, Gregory's, Joy-Den, Apple Hill, Georgia Dachs, Brazos Ski, Brodney, and my own Laddland. If

any of these appear in your pedigrees, you know your
Dachshund comes from a noble heritage and is the result of a
purposeful breeding program.

Today, Dachshunds are shown in three coats and two sizes.
Smooths and Longhairs appear to have developed from the
original strains, though the first Longhair was exhibited at
Crufts in only 1923. Wirehairs are
certainly the most recent addition to
the family.

*Katie is a beautiful
black and tan smooth
Dachshund owned by
Anne Watkins. Smooths
are commonly
considered the most
"Dachshund-like" of the
three varieties.*

Miniatures are the result of
gamekeepers' desires to dwarf their
standards to pursue small game right
into their holes. Developed during the
1800s, these dogs were bred for their
hunting talents alone. By 1934, nine
miniatures were exhibited at the
Dachshund Club of America National Specialty. Breeders of
these dear little dogs had their work cut out for them, they had
to improve their conformation and transform them into
showstars capable of competing against standards. Today, they
frequently win.

Perhaps some of the most recent historical developments
with Dachshunds have stressed sharing bloodlines world-wide.
Surprising as it may be, fewer German than English dogs have
been infused into recent breeding programs. Australian
miniatures are highly prized and appreciated world-wide, as
are the English Draksleat Mini-wires.

Traveling back to America, American Dachshunds are now
believed by many to be the best world-wide. American-bred
dogs are top winners in countries like France, Germany, Spain,
Portugal, and South Africa. Though Europe prefers a smaller
Dachshund than the American
showrings, American Dachshunds'
type and elegance have set them
apart wherever they go.

*Wirehairs are the most recent
addition to the Dachshund family.
The wire coat is the most difficult
of the three coat types to groom
and maintain properly.*

STANDARD for the Dachshund

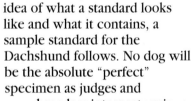

The Dachshund, like all purebred dogs, is measured against a breed standard, a written description of what the ideal specimen should look like. Each dog-registering organization has its own set of standards, one for each of the breeds it recognizes; however, these standards may vary, in the way they are worded, from registry to registry and from country to country. As standards change from time to time on an irregular basis, it is often difficult to keep up with the dog-registering organization's latest approved standard. To give the reader an idea of what a standard looks like and what it contains, a sample standard for the Dachshund follows. No dog will be the absolute "perfect" specimen as judges and breeders interpret various phrases in various ways; hence, it is unlikely that a dog will be judged the same way by two different judges.

Dachshunds are bred in two different sizes and three different coat types. This adorable pup is a miniature Longhair owned by Liz A. Bernel.

GENERAL APPEARANCE

Low to ground, long in body and short of leg with robust muscular development, the skin is elastic and pliable without excessive wrinkling. Appearing neither crippled, awkward, nor cramped in his capacity for movement, the Dachshund is well-balanced with bold and confident head carriage and intelligent, alert facial expression. His hunting spirit, good nose, loud tongue and distinctive build make him well-suited for below-ground work and for beating the bush. His keen nose gives him an advantage over most other breeds for trailing. **Note:** Inasmuch as the Dachshund is a

Ch. Laddland A Wing And A Prayer, co-owned by the author, is a multiple award winner and an excellent breed representative.

hunting dog, scars from honorable wounds shall not be considered a fault.

SIZE, PROPORTION, SUBSTANCE
Bred and shown in two sizes, standard and miniature, miniatures are not a separate classification but compete in a class division for "11 pounds and under at 12 months of age and older." Weight of the standard size is usually between 16 and 32 pounds.

HEAD
Viewed from above or from the side, the head tapers uniformly to the tip of the nose. The eyes are of medium size, almond-shaped and dark-rimmed, with an energetic, pleasant expression; not piercing; very dark in color. The bridge bones over the eyes are strongly prominent. Wall eyes, except in the case of dappled dogs, are a serious fault. The ears are set near

the top of the head, not too far forward, of moderate length, rounded, not narrow, pointed, or folded. Their carriage, when animated, is with the forward edge just touching the cheek so that the ears frame the face. The skull is slightly arched, neither too broad nor too narrow, and slopes gradually with little perceptible stop into the finely-formed, slightly arched muzzle. Black is the preferred color of the nose. Lips are tightly stretched, well covering the lower jaw. Nostrils well open. Jaws opening wide and hinged well back of the eyes, with strongly developed bones and teeth. **Teeth**—Powerful canine teeth; teeth fit closely together in a scissors bite. An even bite is a minor fault. Any other deviation is a serious fault.

Ch. Laddland Pinch of Cameo illustrates "little perceptible stop" and a "finely formed, slightly arched muzzle" as outlined by the standard.

NECK

Long, muscular, clean-cut, without dewlap, slightly arched in the nape, flowing gracefully into the shoulders.

Ch. Pruitt's Red Ripper, owned by Margaret Pruitt, displays the Dacshund's gracefully sloping neck as well as the rich, vibrant, red coat coloration.

TRUNK

The trunk is long and fully muscled. When viewed in profile, the back lies in the straightest possible line between the withers and the short very slightly arched loin. A body that hangs loosely between the shoulders is a serious fault. **Abdomen**—Slightly drawn up.

FOREQUARTERS

For effective underground work, the front must be strong, deep, long and cleanly muscled. Forequarters in detail: **Chest**—The breastbone is strongly prominent in front so that on either side a depression or dimple appears. When viewed from the front, the thorax appears oval and extends downward to the mid-point of the forearm. The enclosing structure of well-sprung ribs appears full and oval to allow, by its ample capacity, complete development of heart and lungs. The keel merges gradually into the line of the abdomen and extends well beyond the front legs. Viewed in profile, the lowest point of the breast line is covered by the front leg. **Shoulder Blades**—Long, broad, well-laid back and firmly placed upon the fully developed thorax, closely fitted at the withers, furnished with hard yet pliable muscles. **Upper Arm**—Ideally the same length as the shoulder blade and at right angles to the latter, strong of bone and hard of muscle, lying close to the ribs, with elbows close to the body, yet capable of free movement. **Forearm**—Short; supplied with hard yet pliable muscles on the front and outside, with tightly stretched tendons on the inside and at the back, slightly curved inwards. The joints between the forearms and the feet (wrists) are closer together than the shoulder joints, so that the front does not appear absolutely straight. Knuckling over is a disqualifying fault. **Feet**—Front paws are full, tight, compact, with well-arched toes and tough, thick pads.

To clearly visualize Dachshund type as set forth by the standard, take a look at a Westminster winner! Ch. Luvadox Rose Parade is owner/ handled by Gina Leone.

They may be equally inclined a trifle outward. There are five toes, four in use, close together with a pronounced arch and strong, short nails. Front dewclaws may be removed.

HINDQUARTERS

Strong and cleanly muscled. The pelvis, the thigh, the second thigh, and the metatarsus are ideally the same length and form a series of right angles. From the rear, the thighs are strong and powerful. The legs turn neither in nor out. **Metatarsus**–Short and strong, perpendicular to the second thigh bone. When viewed from behind, they are upright and parallel. **Feet**–Hind Paws–Smaller than the front paws with four compactly closed and arched toes with tough, thick pads. The entire foot points straight ahead and is balanced equally on the ball and not merely on the toes. Rear dewclaws should be removed. **Croup**–Long, rounded and full, sinking slightly toward the tail. **Tail**– Set in continuation of the spine, extending without kinks, twists, or pronounced curvature, and not carried too gaily.

The Dachshund's gait should be smooth, with good reach in the front. In order to achieve adequate reach, the dog needs proper shoulder assembly to compensate for his short legs.

GAIT

Fluid and smooth. Forelegs reach well forward, without much lift, in unison with the driving action of hind legs. The correct shoulder assembly and well-fitted elbows allow the long, free stride in front. Viewed from the front, the legs do not move in exact parallel planes, but incline slightly inward to compensate for shortness of leg and width of chest. Hind legs drive on a line with the forelegs, with hocks (metatarsus) turning neither in nor out. The propulsion of the hind leg depends on the dog's ability to carry the hind leg to complete extension. Viewed in profile, the forward reach of the hind leg equals the rear extension. The thrust of correct movement is seen when the rear pads are clearly exposed during rear extension. Feet must travel parallel to the line of motion with no tendency to swing out, cross over, or interfere with each other. Short, choppy movement, rolling or high-stepping gait, close or overly wide coming or going are incorrect. The Dachshund must have agility, freedom of movement, and endurance to do the work for which he was developed.

TEMPERAMENT

The Dachshund is clever, lively and courageous to the point of rashness, persevering in above and below ground work, with all the senses well-developed. Any display of shyness is a serious fault.

SPECIAL CHARACTERISTICS OF THE THREE COAT VARIETIES

The Dachshund is bred with three varieties of coat: (1) Smooth; (2) Wirehaired; (3) Longhaired and is shown in two sizes, standard and miniature. All three varieties and both sizes must conform to the characteristics already specified. The following features are applicable for each variety:

Smooth Dachshund

Coat–Short, smooth and shining. Should be neither too long nor too thick. Ears not leathery. **Tail**–Gradually tapered to a point, well but not too richly haired. Long sleek bristles on the underside are considered a patch of strong-growing hair, not a fault. A brush tail is a fault, as is also a partly or wholly hairless tail. **Color of Hair**–Although base color is immaterial, certain patterns and basic colors predominate. One-colored Dachshunds include red (with or without a shading of interspersed dark hairs or sable) and cream. A small amount of white on the chest is acceptable, but not desirable. **Nose and nails**–black.

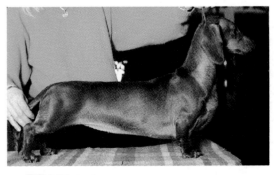

Ch. Laddland Just A Taste is a former National Specialty Best of Breed winner. She is a smooth Dachshund with red coat coloration.

Two-colored Dachshunds include black, chocolate, wild boar, gray (blue) and fawn (Isabella), each with tan markings over the eyes, on the sides of the jaw and underlip, on the inner edge of the ear, front, breast, inside and behind the front legs, on the paws and around the anus, and from there to about one-third to one-half of the length of the tail on the underside. Undue prominence or extreme lightness of tan markings is undesirable. A small amount of white on the chest is acceptable but not desirable. **Nose and**

Black Dachshunds have tan markings on various parts of the body. Ch. Bridger's Sunny Shurbert gives Georjan Bridger a big Dachshund kiss.

Even the most playful pups need to take a break now and then! A pile of dozing eight-week-old standard Smooth pups owned by Gina and Patricia Leone.

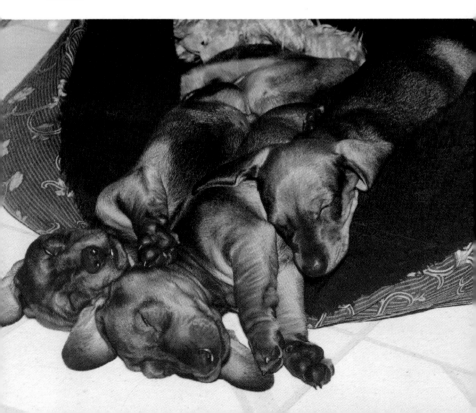

nails–in the case of black dogs, black; for chocolate and all other colors, dark brown, but self-colored is acceptable.

Dappled Dachshunds–The "single" dapple pattern is expressed as lighter-colored areas contrasting with the darker base color, which may be any acceptable color. Neither the light nor the dark color should predominate. Nose and nails are the same as for one and two-colored Dachshunds. Partial or wholly blue (wall) eyes are as acceptable as dark eyes. A large area of white on the chest of a dapple is permissible.

A "double" dapple is one in which varying amounts of white coloring occur over the body in addition to the dapple pattern. **Nose and nails**– as for one and two-color Dachshunds; partial or wholly self-colored is permissible.

The wirehaired Dachshund is covered with a thick, rough outer coat and a somewhat softer undercoat. His distinguishing facial furnishings include a beard and wiry eyebrows.

Brindle is a pattern (as opposed to a color) in which black or dark stripes occur over the entire body although in some specimens the pattern may be visible only in the tan points.

Wirehaired Dachshund

Coat–With the exception of jaw, eyebrows, and ears, the whole body is covered with a uniform tight, short, thick, rough, hard, outer coat but with finer, somewhat softer, shorter hairs (undercoat) everywhere distributed between the coarser hairs. The absence of an undercoat is a fault. The distinctive facial furnishings include a beard and eyebrows. On the ears the hair is shorter than on the body, almost smooth. The general arrangement of the hair is such that the wirehaired Dachshund, when viewed from a distance, resembles the smooth. Any sort of soft hair in the outercoat, wherever found on the body, especially on the top of the head, is a fault. The same is true of long, curly, or wavy hair, or hair that sticks out irregularly in all directions. **Tail**–Robust, thickly haired, gradually tapering to a point. A flag tail is a fault. **Color of Hair**–While the most common colors are wild boar, black and tan, and various shades of red, all colors are admissible. A small amount of white on the chest, although acceptable, is not desirable. **Nose and nails**–same as for the smooth variety.

Longhaired Dachshund

Coat–The sleek, glistening, often slightly wavy hair is longer under the neck and on the forechest, the underside of the body, the ears, and behind the legs. The coat gives the dog an elegant appearance. Short hair on the ear is not desirable. Too profuse a coat which masks type, equally long hair over the whole body, a curly coat, or a pronounced parting on the back are faults. **Tail**–Carried gracefully in prolongation of the spine; the hair attains its greatest length here and forms a veritable flag. **Color of Hair**–Same as for the smooth Dachshund. **Nose and nails**–same as for the smooth.

The foregoing description is that of the ideal Dachshund. Any deviation from the above described dog must be penalized to the extent of the deviation keeping in mind the importance of the contribution of the various features toward the basic original purpose of the breed.

True Dachshund type should always shine through, regardless of coat color or variety.

DISQUALIFICATIONS
Knuckling over of front legs.

COMMENTS ON THE STANDARD
In our previous standard, the term ram's nose was used. This description was removed from our new standard for two reasons. First, it was not what was being seen regularly in the show ring today; a straighter nose line was emerging as the norm. Second, there was some confusion associated with using a term that mentions another animal. Even though the term is no longer used, a ram's nose, or Roman nose, is appreciated by Dachshund lovers and breeders.

The longhaired Dachshund's sleek wavy hair gives it an elegant appearance. Longhairs are seen in the same colors as Smooths.

There is no color disqualification in Dachshunds. Any color is acceptable.

The Dachshund is exemplified by its long body, low profile, and prominent forechest. This fluid body line and forechest should be visible in movement, as well as when standing.

DECIDING on a Dachshund

D id you pick a Dachshund for its sense of humor? Did you pick a Dachshund because it is an easy-care dog with no need for extensive grooming? Did you pick a Dachshund because it combines the spirit of a larger hunting dog and the small, child-safe physique that is unique only to the Dachshund? Did you want a dog with a lot of personality that doesn't require a lot of physical control? However it happened, you've decided on a Dachshund. This is only the first of your new decisions.

Dachshunds mean choices. In the United States, Dachshunds come in three coat varieties and two sizes. In Europe, there are actually three sizes to make the choices even more difficult. Let's start with size.

Some people may be drawn to the Dachshund because of its small size. This Smooth puppy loves to be "babied"—he especially likes to be pushed in his stroller.

STANDARDS VERSUS MINIATURES

A miniature is 11 pounds and under at one year of age or older. Miniatures were developed by breeders to provide a petite hunter capable of chasing rabbits right down their holes and into their dens.

Miniatures have major size advantages for apartment dwellers, older Dachshund lovers and those whose living arrangements offer limited space. Remember, a miniature is 11 pounds and under, if it's a real miniature. Unfortunately,

The Dachshund is a breed with definite personality. Ch. Dachsborough Nedrum, CDX, is a real "hot dog" on his skateboard—he loves the attention!

Hey...what's that on my head? This miniature puppy is not much bigger than an autumn leaf, and a true miniature Dachshund won't exceed 11 pounds at age one.

there are tons of people out there who want the higher price asked for a miniature but will give you a dog that will grow to be as much as 14 to 16 pounds. These aren't miniatures and are *not* what any respectable breeder is aiming to produce.

If a good breeder has an off-size Dachshund, he should tell you so and you can factor this into your decision. If you have any dream of showing your dog, these off-size specimens won't suit your long-term needs. You can always ask a breeder to weigh a dog or its parents for you, and most good breeders can estimate how big most dogs will be.

The full-size Dachshund is called a standard and can be expected to grow to between 16 and 35 pounds. Females tend to be at the lower end of the scale and males at the higher end. But take it from someone who knows, it would be very hard to finish a bitch who weighs 16 pounds. Ideal show weights for standards are 19 to 25 pounds for a female and 26 to 31 pounds for a male.

COAT VARIETIES

Longhairs tend to be the largest of the coat varieties and some exceed 35 pounds. The new American Kennel Club breed standard encourages longhairs to fall more into the size of wires and smooths. Of the three varieties, smooth Dachshunds tend to be the smallest. They are sleeker in every way. Wirehairs, which have terrier-like whiskers and beards, tend to be in the middle.

Smooths

Most people are familiar only with the smooth Dachshund, and, perhaps, it is the most "Dachshund" of the three varieties. I believe that smooths were the original variety with occasional recessive longhairs.

It is believed that the smooth coat was the original Dachshund coat variety. This pair of Laddland Smooths creates a striking profile.

In temperament, smooths are the most artistic. They select what *they* want to do. The Dachshund is a very smart dog that needed its intellect to direct it into which badger tunnel would house a badger and not a dead-end where the dog could be trapped. When you start with this type of intelligence, the dog can be expected to select what *it* likes to do. Like every German stereotype, smooths are stubborn, determined and opinionated. Unlike any German stereotype, the occasional fault of smooths is shyness. Uniquely, this is an American problem that goes back to their original Dachshund forefathers. In several parts of Europe, the shyest Dachshunds are longhairs.

Smooths require the least amount of grooming and will almost always satisfy the needs of those who are allergic as long as the dog is bathed every month. For people like myself who appreciate the sheer physical beauty of a Dachshund, there is no more precise example of the breed than the smooth. You can't hide its faults—what you see is what you've got. For this reason, I respond to the challenge of breeding dogs that need to be as correct as possible because there is very little you can hide from the eyes of a knowledgeable judge.

Smooths are the most vulnerable to the assaults of cold and wet weather. Dachshunds can be attacked on all four sides by bad weather. When you're only 5 to 9 inches high at the shoulder, you're vulnerable to the bounce-back effect of rain hitting the ground and then you. When you are a smooth, you have no extra hair to defend you against the elements. Don't be surprised if your smart smooth feigns that it is just impossible to go out in terrible weather. Forget it. Remember, Dachshunds will always try to train you their way. Force them to go out but don't make them stay out there long.

Longhairs

Longhairs are the most laid-back of the Dachshunds yet they are frequently the most avid hunters and racers. Their coats demand more grooming but give them a theatrical dominance that makes them appear to flow across a show ring. Don't think that when they are described as laid-back that they will bark less, as they certainly don't.

Longhairs are popular showdogs, as their coats add to their appeal. Clever grooming, as with any coated breed, can

Ch. Saytar's Rock of Gibraltar has the poise and flowing beauty of a longhaired Dachshund.

disguise faults and enhance good points. For these reasons, today, in America, there are more longhair entries than the other two varieties.

Like any dog with a coat, you'll need to bathe your longhair every three to four weeks and brush a bit every day. If you want to show, you'll be bathing every other week and really caring for your dog's coat; get a breeder in your area to help you.

Just like the statue, this Siddach's standard Longhair puppy is a work of art. Owned by Sidney Stafford.

Three generations of Longhairs—Ch. Solong Squire v Bristleknoll on the right, his son Ch. Amtekel's the Great Gatsby on the left, and his black and tan son in the center.

Wirehairs

Wirehairs are the least known and the newest of the three varieties. To get the rough coat desired for hunting and surviving brambles and burrs of the forests, Dachshunds were crossed with terriers. The result was a Dachshund with the fire and brimstone natural to a terrier and

the intellect and long, low body of a Dachshund.

There is rarely anything shy about this variety. They are the "macho men" and "spirited ladies" who never let you forget that they love any confrontation.

Their rough, double coat spares them from dealing with the roughest elements and protects them from injury. Yet, if you want to show your wirehair, you'll need to learn quite a bit about grooming. These dogs cannot be clipped for show; they must be hand stripped and plucked like a terrier. However, if showing isn't a concern, you can expect that the wire coat will survive on its own even if the coveted beard and brows don't.

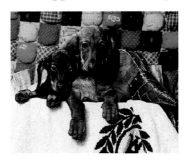

Black with tan markings and red are the two coat color varieties most commonly seen in the Dachshund.

DACHSHUNDS COME IN MANY COLORS

The two most common colors for Dachshunds are red and black and tan. Red Dachshunds range from strawberry blonde to dark brown with an overlay of black and a widow's peak. Black and tans are primarily black with tan brows, mouth makeup, feet, tail base and derriere and cheek rear dimples. Though any of the varieties can come in any color, wirehairs also come in a coat called wild boar that mixes hairs that range from gray to buff brown.

In the category called two-color Dachshunds, black and tan is the most common. Other possibilities include chocolate and tan, Isabella (fawn-colored) and blue. All come with their tan markings and dark or self-colored noses and eyes.

Pucker up and get ready...here I come! This miniature Wirehair pup isn't shy about public displays of affection when it comes to his favorite toy.

Then there are dapples. Here two or three colors are mixed much as they are on a blue merle Collie. The extreme of this coloration is called a double dapple where there are also large sections of white in the markings. And this isn't all. Dapples come in any of the color

31

families: black and tan, chocolate and tan and red.

This isn't even the end of the color story. Rarely seen piebalds are one or two colors and white. Creams, primarily from European or Australian origin, boast of Palomino hair but with dark noses and eyes. Many other color possibilities exist in Dachshunds, but many are color dilutes and come from less-than-perfect breeding where other genetic problems can be expected as well.

If you want an unusually colored Dachshund, please go to a breeder respected for his knowledge in this area. Do not go to anyone merely "dabbling" in color.

Is This the Right Time for You to Have a Dog?

Once you've lived with and loved a dog, you should know when you're ready for another one. If this is the case, you will never replace your old dog but you can have a new friend with a new personality and new special talents and needs.

Strangely enough, I find that people forget that they will need to retrain their new dog and how much work it is. You and your dog probably had 14 years together and you both trained each other. Now you will be starting with a baby who doesn't know anything, not even you. Training takes time and love blooms over time.

Developing a relationship with a dog is much like developing a good marriage. It won't be done overnight and it won't be done without you and your dog spending an enjoyable amount of time together.

First-time dog owners are more likely not to know when is the right time to get a dog. A dog is as much work as having another child. If you're not prepared for that, don't do it.

Let's say someone has a young family with two children under the age of seven. The husband is starting a new business and the wife is helping. I wouldn't want them to have one of my dogs.

If you can't guarantee that you'll plan to spend one hour of quality time a day with your dog, why do you want one? By quality time I mean walking your dog, sitting with him on the floor, playing games with him and encouraging him to play with other members of your family.

Children under the age of seven aren't prepared to understand when they are being rough with puppies. Their body language is threatening to dogs; leaning over and squealing at any dog will upset it. I have found young children trying to pick my dogs up by their ears. Many children just don't understand what hurts toys, dogs or humans and they make a game of finding out. Think of all the times a child has pinched your arm to test you.

When a child is old enough to take on the responsibility of some of the dog's care is when he is old enough for a dog. Otherwise, it is the adult's responsibility to protect the dog from the child.

A Dachshund (or two!) can make a wonderful pet if the time and effort is taken to make the dog a well-behaved member of the family.

Now if you understand that you must devote time to your pet and expect a tough training period and a few chewed shoes before your Dachshund becomes your best friend, then you're ready to proceed.

OWNING a Dachshund

I didn't grow up wanting a Dachshund. No, I liked "big" dogs and sporting dogs. My family had other ideas. We had a family meeting, and the only access we had to good breeders gave us the choices of a Dachshund or a Standard Poodle. Everyone else voted for the Dachshund. I was 15 and I refused to be seen with this long low dog for about a week. Since then I have never lived a week of my life without a least one Dachshund. I fell for the breed's complete devotion and loyalty and I was mesmerized by its sense of humor. Anyone who has loved a

Dachshunds are known for their sense of humor and unique personality—they will do just about anything for attention. This "cowboy" is Ch. Dachsborough Nedrum, CDX.

Dachshunds often like to cuddle up on the furniture if their owners allow it. Elsa and Ingrid snuggle in a cozy corner of the couch. Courtesy of Model Team, Ocean Grove, NJ.

Dachshund will mention its humor. Dachshunds love to be the center of attention. They are smart enough to revel in a spot of honor and enjoy figuring out how to attain it. They will perform tricks, wear clothes, learn what delights you or what annoys you and repeat it regularly in a humorous way.

A Dachshund follows in your footsteps. Don't step back from the mirror without looking behind you because that is where your pet will be, waiting to follow you wherever you go. Dachshunds love their owners and pick members of the family to be favored with their devotion. They don't give this devotion immediately! They must be won over. They say things like, "let's talk about this" and "let me think this over." Dachshunds have opinions on almost every topic and you will know them. Don't think your Dachshund will love all of your friends as you do. They will shop through your friends to see which ones will achieve favors and which ones will be ignored, or worse, deemed not necessary.

Dachshunds make wonderful bed-dogs. They love to burrow down under the covers and most will cuddle like bedbugs.

Unfortunately, if your Dachshund sleeps across the bed, and many do, you are going to be cramped for space.

Dachshunds sound like big dogs from the other side of a door. They are very protective and any Dachshund worth its feisty persistence will defend his master or his master's hearth and home.

I owned one Dachshund who was afraid of nuns and Volkswagens; shapes that were unique threw him. He also loved to let me get ahead while walking him and then he'd flip on his back and thump his tail to attract as much attention as possible from anyone passing by.

I have another Dachshund who kisses and hugs like a human being. His mother goes to work with me every day and leads those who visit my store to her dog biscuit box where she turns into a pointer. She says hello, come and no, just the sort of words you'd expect a Dachshund to say.

Is this what "puppy love" is all about? Ch. Siddach's Aria gets a big kiss from her young daughter, Siddach's Diva.

Your Dachshund will find unique ways to please and amuse you. It is simply the Dachshund thing to do. But everything about Dachshunds isn't perfect.

Dachshunds love to hunt. Mice, rabbits, chipmunks and squirrels are meant to be chased according to a Dachshund. If a Dachshund brings you one of these as a gift, it is natural for them to do so. It is up to you to decide what to do about it.

Many Dachshunds dig. Remember they were bred to go down holes. Of the 30 or 40 Dachshunds I've owned, I've had three or four diggers and only one who is truly an excavator. To make it all the more confusing, I can tell you that nary a mother, grandmother or great grandmother of these dogs had any interest in the digging sport. Keep your dog busy playing with other things, this appears to be your best defense against this bad habit.

Dachshunds have no sense about eating—they never know when to stop. Feeding your Dachshund controlled portions at specific times will keep him from "pigging out."

Dachshunds seem to have no sense about cars or traffic. They love to ride in cars but they seem to not even see them. It's almost like they think cars are in a different reality.

Therefore, you must train your dog to stay away from traffic, or even more practically, just keep your dog away from traffic situations. Only be around cars when your dog is on a leash and under your control. Even when a car pulls up slowly into a driveway, Dachshunds don't seem to realize they're in danger. Be the protector for your dog and keep him away from the situation.

Dachshunds are pigs. Don't leave open bags of dog food or trash cans where Dachshunds can get to them. Dachshunds were bred to make a kill once a week and gorge themselves. They have no sense about eating and have no idea when to stop. Keep food and trash cans covered. I've literally had people call me after these types of accidents, and one dog had to have its stomach pumped to save its life.

Dachshunds can destroy most toys. Avoid things that can clog in their throats or choke them. Use Nylabone® and soft fleece toys. The latter they will de-squeak and unstuff but then they'll love them.

A FENCED YARD EASES LIFE WITH ANY DOG

My theme song is fence them in. Your back yard is more than a bathroom for your dog. It is also a playground and a place where he can hunt and run. Dachshunds love to do all of these things. They don't need an acre or even a half acre. I don't even have my entire back yard fenced. I have about one third of it fenced. This cuts down on barking as dogs bark more when they are protecting the boundary when a neighbor is standing on his property 5 feet away.

The best fenced area is one that is long and wide enough so that the dog can run comfortably in ovals. This means that the area doesn't demand that a dog stop and turn. (Remember, we are designing the best alternative, not just a 20-by-8-foot survival run.) Next, this area should present a variety of footings. We all know that cement footing is the easiest to clean and hose down but it also gets very hot in sunny weather and encourages flat feet for any dog. You could have one area cement and another area dirt or gravel. Now the minute you have dirt, you must plan to clean up feces. You don't want to take any chance of getting parasites into your soil or you are likely to have them for eternity.

How Do You Fence The Area?

Chain link fence is the best and, if you have visible neighbors, you may want to back it up with stockade "view blocking" fence on the outside. And if you are doing this the best way possible, sparing no expense, you will have a trench dug and drop the fence a couple of inches into the soil. Also, in

A chain link fence is the best way to keep your Dachshund safe in your yard, but extra measures must be taken so that he cannot dig his way out.

the same vein, make sure the gates are close to the ground. For true safety, dig below the gates and fill in with bricks or cement blocks.

The final safety trick is to take railroad ties and line the base of your chain link fence on the outside everywhere you don't have stockade fence. Here you may just want to reinforce with some cement blocks.

Now why do you think we do all this? We're planning a safe retreat for a breed that has a tendency to dig.

Even a Dachshund that has a fenced-in area to play in won't be happy without human companionship. Remember that Dachshunds thrive on attention from their owners.

What About Electric Fences?

Electric fences only scare off the dog that is wearing the electronic collar that is catching the shock waves. Your neighbor's giant dog can walk right in. So can raccoons and skunks and cats and rabbits, which your dog would love to chase.

My second concern with these fences is that their shocks are too extreme for smart little Dachshunds. They don't understand where this punishment is coming from and some will react with increased nervousness.

Now if someone has a ten-acre homestead, the dog will probably rarely come in contact with the fence or visitors who have crossed the line. Here these fences may be appropriate for those who don't want to see their fences.

How Long Should You Leave Your Dog Outside?

In any fenced area, you should be sure there is a shaded or protected area where your dog can escape any time he is left out for more than an hour in good weather.

While your dog is out for more than an hour, you should also be sure water is available. And be sure the water is fresh and changed each day. You can't leave water outside for a day without it turning into a bug trap.

In cold weather, I believe, no dog should be left out for more than an hour. Smooths will let you know they don't want to spend nearly that amount of time out in despicable weather.

Remember, they don't have the coats that longs and wires do to defend them against the elements.

As you already know, it is wise to clean up after your dog every day or every other day. First, no dog wants to stay in a limited area with his own feces. Secondly, it isn't healthy for anyone. And finally, some dogs will eat it. Either bury it in a selected corner or double bag it and throw it in the trash or find some other area of your yard that will benefit from natural fertilizer.

In summary, second to a loving owner or family, nothing improves the quality of life of a Dachshund like his own fenced area. It gives him a playroom, bathroom, exercise room, and hunting area. Fenced areas make Dachshunds and Dachshund owners happy campers.

WHAT DO DACHSHUNDS EAT?

Dachshunds have as close to cast iron stomachs as any breed. Yet, they seem to bloom best under a basic diet that utilizes a nutritionally complete kibble dog food with a protein count of 25 percent or less.

When I question things, I always go back to what would have been the best natural diet for a dog. They would not eat solely meat. They would eat a variety of things that would cut the protein content of a total meat diet. I mix kibble with water and a tablespoon of canned meat for dogs. As a treat, I give my dogs an occasional tablespoon of cottage cheese or yogurt and I sometimes add tablescraps.

Years ago, I fed my pet dogs only meat. When they were old, I had terrible trouble with their teeth and one even lost his canines. I believe I influenced that by feeding only canned meat.

Each breeder and each veterinarian have their own viewpoints about diet. The most important thing to remember is that no dog should be underfed or overfed. Any food that says it is 100% complete is nutritious.

FUTURE CONSIDERATIONS FOR YOUR DACHSHUND

Competition

Dachshunds are eligible for many different types of competitions. You could spend every day of your life preparing or doing some sort of Dachshund competition if you and your dog had the persistence to do so.

1. Show conformation judging. There should be kennel clubs in your area that sponsor handling classes as preparation for these events. Hopefully, you also have a local Dachshund club that can help you find shows in your area.

2. Obedience. This is the most basic behavior training and it is the easiest to find in almost any area. Good obedience classes will cover the basics right up to scent discrimination.

What do Dachshunds eat...more appropriately, what don't they eat? Your veterinarian or breeder can advise you about a nutritionally balanced diet for your Dachshund.

3. Field trials. Dachshund clubs will need to inform you about these. Here you take your dog out in a field and test his tracking and hunting instincts against peer Dachshunds.

4. Den trials. These are held for both Dachshunds and terriers. They may be sponsored by either Dachshund or terrier clubs such as the AWTA (American Working Terrier Association). These events test a dog's instinct to go into dens, make turns and confront prey.

5. Earth Dog Test. This is one of the newest tests and evaluates a dog's tracking and hunting skills. As it is very new, I have only heard of Dachshund clubs offering this test, but I would expect it will become popular in the near future.

6. Canine Good Citizen Test. This is an AKC (American Kennel Club) program designed to offer dogs with good basic obedience behavior a special award. This is done

mostly for fun but may be a criteria to be eligible for therapy work with children, senior citizens, and handicapped people.

7. Agility. This is an obstacle course designed for dogs to test their intelligence and coordination.

Breeding

In today's environment no breeder will encourage a pet owner to breed his dog. Leave it to those of us who know what we are doing and how to find good homes for our offspring. If you obtain conformation titles, obedience titles or den or field trial championships on your dog and wish to breed, there will be people involved with those endeavors who will help you make breeding plans.

If you are only interested in breeding a pet dog, you need to go back to the breeder from whom you obtained the dog. If anyone will help you, this is the person.

If you want to breed your female, I always tell people that they must be prepared for the following possibilities.

1. To have a veterinarian ready to give a Cesarean if needed and have the money to pay for it. The procedure costs between $200 and $1,000.

2. To bottle feed an entire litter if required. I figure 15 minutes a puppy and puppies need to be fed every three hours for the first three to four days.

3. To keep an entire litter until you find homes for them. This frequently takes six or seven months and breeders should be on lists where people call for puppies.

4. To possibly lose the dog if things don't all go well.

That irresistible Dachshund "puppy cuteness" may influence your desire to try your hand at breeding, but it is not a decision to be rushed into or taken lightly.

Today all of us who love Dachshunds are involved with Dachshund Rescue. This involves accepting Dachshunds people no longer want, evaluating them, having them altered and then placed in homes where they are more appreciated. These efforts are supported by the Dachshund Club of America, Inc., and are its way of helping humane efforts everywhere.

Anyone who breeds a litter may need to master the art of bottle feeding. Newborn puppies need to be fed every three hours for their first three or four days.

Breeders only want the very best for their breed and, therefore, believe in breeding only high-quality dogs. This trio of roughhousing Laddland puppies was bred by the author.

We all want to breed better, healthier dogs. Today, when so many dogs are unwanted, breeders believe all Dachshunds should be loved and only the very best should be bred.

HOUSEBREAKING Your New Puppy

If you think there is one successful way to housebreak a dog that always works, you are wrong. However, there are two words associated with every successful result. Those words are consistency and rewards. I believe puppies really don't have complete control until somewhere between four and six months of age. I also believe small dogs seem to be slower to develop control than most large breeds. Housebreaking Dachshunds is not the easiest thing that anyone who loves them has done, but you can, and will, be successful.

Keep in mind a dog defecates or urinates within an hour of eating or drinking water. One never removes water from a dog, but his drinking can be controlled, especially after 7 p.m. if you're going to crate your puppy.

The most important thing is to think of how are you going to make "going out" a pleasurable experience within an hour of your dog's eating? You will go back to this rule regularly during the housebreaking of your dog.

THE PUPPY SHOPPING LIST

Here are the most basic things you'll need to greet your new puppy.

1. An 8 to 20 lb. bag of whatever puppy food your puppy has been raised eating.

2. Bottled water. Later, once he's passed the stress of moving into your house, you can

Food and water bowls are necessary accessories for your new puppy, even though seven-week-old Laddland City Sizzle has invented a different use for hers.

switch him to your tap water.

3. A collar for walks. I would expect your puppy will need a 12-inch choke collar. I prefer these, as they aid in training and a puppy can't slip it over his head like the regular band collar.

There are many preparations to be made in order to give your new "baby" a proper homecoming.

4. A 6-foot leash, approximately a half-inch wide with the smallest hook you can find.

5. A crate that will be big enough for your Dachshund when he is full grown.

6. Some form of bedding. Fleece pads, which are easy to launder, are the best. Cotton rugs or blankets are acceptable as well.

7. A water bowl. The best are ceramic because dogs don't pick them up and move them.

8. A 1-quart food bowl, either stainless steel or pottery. Do not pick steep, deep bowls as Dachshunds must stick their

noses way to the base. A regularly rounded bowl is best.

9. A pile of newspapers, large ones and rolls of paper towels.

10. Toys. Rubber squeak toys only seem to survive with young puppies though they are dangerous at any age. Nylabones® and Gumabones® are good throughout a dog's lifetime. You can use good rawhide toys such as Roar-Hide™ by Nylabone® when you are there supervising. When I leave dogs in crates, I like to give them a special toy for that quiet time.

11. The name of a good veterinarian who you can get to easily if you need his assistance.

THE YOUNG PUPPY (UNDER FIVE MONTHS)

Puppies relieve themselves when they wake up and after they eat. Within an hour after they eat, most dogs will urinate or defecate. Puppies simply do everything faster and more often. After all, they eat three times a day.

Here is the most basic training plan:

1. Take your puppy out as soon as he wakes up. When he relieves himself, praise him. And if you want to help cement the memory give a little treat. Say "good dog" or add the dog's name.

2. After you feed your puppy, take him out again. Then watch your puppy's timing and schedule. If it takes him 20 minutes to go, the next time you can take him out ten minutes after eating. If you don't mind a lifetime of treats, give him one as a reward after he eliminates. If a lifetime of praise is easier, *sell the praise.* Let your puppy know you love him and are pleased with what he is doing. If you don't let him know this pleases you, he will have two playrooms: one is inside and one is outside, and he'll go to the bathroom in either place.

Treats can be given as a reward for a job well done but they are no substitute for your love and lots of praise.

3. When you take your puppy back in the house and he has both urinated and defecated, you know he can safely wander the house for a limited period of time.

Of course you, the head dog, will supervise this free time to make sure he doesn't get into puppy mischief.

4. Before you go to bed, take your puppy out. If he is going to be crated, it gives him yet another chance to not have to hold it for the evening. Just like humans, a little exercise will encourage things to move through the system with healthy speed.

At this age, this trip out may be as much for you physically as it is for the puppy. Later, when he is an adult, this will be an important trip. Remember, consistency was one of our key words, so we start this ritual at a young age but it will be most appreciated once the dog has full control of his bodily functions.

While your dog is this young, he may train you when he needs to go out. When you see a dog start to sniff around and circle, if you are not already outside, get there as quickly as possible.

A FENCED YARD AIDS TRAINING

A fenced yard with an explorable area is the best possible situation for you and your Dachshund. To start with, you will accompany your puppy out on each trip so you can praise him and know when he is "safe" to roam freely back in the house. Once your dog is trained, you won't need to stand out there and wait for him but he'll still like it when you do.

If a young dog doesn't go when you take him out, you must crate him when you take him back inside. Wait half an hour and then take him out again. This is the only way to be successful. When he goes, he can then safely and freely roam as a reward.

Remember one of the keys to good housebreaking is to make it enjoyable for the dog to go out. A fenced yard gives him the most wondrous place to hunt, play, exercise and eliminate.

The only safe alternative to a fenced area is a long walk. Dachshunds are hunters. They can't safely be left free to roam. If you don't have a fenced yard or a fenced area, you *must* do walks. These walks should become enjoyable for both you and your dog. They will become escapes from the mundane, workaholic life we all lead. And they will be your dog's time to explore and be with you as much as they are his chances to do his duties.

Of course, you will need to bring plastic bags to clean up when you walk in almost any setting unless you're lucky enough to never leave your own property.

If you are a city person, stick these plastic bags in your pocket and start walking your young puppy on streets where there isn't tons of traffic to distract or frighten him. Give him plenty of time to sniff and enjoy himself. When he goes, give him all the verbal "good dog" or whatever treats you've decided upon.

When you walk your dog, I suggest the smallest hook, narrowest leads that don't drag under a Dachshund's short legs. It is such a simple concept, short leash hooks for short legs, but it is very helpful. To encourage your dog to exercise as well, when he is older, you can move him up to a flexible lead that permits him to wander 20 feet away and feel that he is truly free and hunting on his own. As wonderful as these leads are don't ever let a dog have too much free reign close to traffic. And don't let your dog explore dense areas where wild animals, like skunks, may be waiting to cause you and your dog real agony.

SPECIAL HOUSEBREAKING HINTS

At night, you can remove water for the evening or around 7 p.m. if you are going to crate your dog. As he's had water close at hand all day, this will only give him several hours where water won't be available. This will help him stay clean and comfortable throughout the night. He wants that just as much as you do.

Not only does a fenced-in yard provide your Dachshund with a safe area to play in, it can also help to simplify the task of housebreaking.

Males are generally easier to train than bitches. Why is that? Well, when puberty hits, and frequently even before, a male will go where a female

has gone. He is claiming the spot. Therefore, if you send your male puppy to an expert to train, the trainer will probably do something simple like walk him with a female. Once she goes, he goes.

I've never found an equally easy route to train a female, but even here, they will frequently go close to where someone else has gone. Walk two dogs together or see if you can find a friendly dog to help you train your puppy. Letting your puppy see everyone praise the other dog when it goes helps too. Puppy see, puppy do.

Consistency means do the same thing repeatedly. If you decide to take your dog out at 7 a.m., don't expect him to wait until 9 a.m. on Sunday. If you go out every three hours, keep it up or crate your puppy or keep it in a confined area with papers. An adult may be able to hold it for six to eight hours but puppies do not.

SHOULD YOU PAPER TRAIN?

All of my dogs are paper trained when they are puppies. This means they will go on basically two sections of a large newspaper. Paper training gives the dog an acceptable alternative when you know you won't be home at the proper hour and he is free in a confined area like a kitchen. It also gives you an alternative when there is 3 feet of snow or you are completely indisposed and can't consider your nightly walk.

The only problem with paper training is when they get so attached to papers that they won't go outside. You may have to take a section of urine-fragranced but dry paper with you to the street to help the dog make the proper association.

Paper training is an acceptable method of housebreaking, but if the puppy becomes used to eliminating on the papers, you may have some trouble getting him to "go" outside.

Puppies Five Months and Up

Now your Dachshund has more control. You may or may not still need to run right out the door in the morning but you know your dog by now. If you have a fenced yard, your dog should go out first thing each morning but by now he probably can go out alone. You no longer need to stand there to encourage and reward him.

During housebreaking, your puppy should only be allowed to roam around the house (supervised, of course) after you are sure that he has relieved himself.

If you are walking your dog, you may now be able to leave your dog crated until you feed him breakfast and then go for your walk.

Four times a day is a good rule of thumb for going out. As your dog matures, you will know if he defecates once or twice a day. Urination is a bit harder to figure. Any dog who drinks a lot of water will urinate more. In later life, your dog may even only need to go out three times a day.

In two weeks, a five or six month old puppy should be successfully housebroken, but you can't let your guard down for a minute. Give him slack for a day and you must add many days to fulfilling your desire to housebreak this cute little dog.

If Success Alludes You, Resort to Crate Training

During this phase, your puppy will be crated except when you know he is safe and has urinated and defecated outside.

1. Take him out the second he wakes up in the morning. Keep the hour consistent.
2. Once you have seen him go, reward him with a treat or verbal praise. Only then can the puppy be loose in the room where you are.
3. Feed him breakfast, if he's still on a breakfast schedule.
4. Within an hour, take him out again.
5. Hopefully your dog will defecate either upon waking or after breakfast. If not, you must be able to watch him indoors to see the circling or sniffing clues that tell you he needs to go out.
6. If the dog does not urinate, he must go back in his crate

and you must take him out in another half hour or so.

7. Once he goes, profess great praise and give rewards.

8. Take him out regularly throughout the day and again after dinner.

9. Dogs who have done both may be trusted up to two hours, depending on their age, to roam free in your house.

10. Don't forget the pre-sleep trip outdoors.

11. Put him to bed in the crate. For camaraderie you can put the crate next to your bed. And what do you have in the crate? Hopefully a soft fleece pad that lets liquid flow through so no dog has to stay on a wet rug. Papers are something to avoid in crates—as you may not have paper trained your puppy but your breeder may have done so. Don't confuse him, soft fleece pads are the best.

You can place fleece pads over a towel or rug or a grate, which is the best base for any crate. A grate lets any liquid seep below and the combination of a fleece pad and grate aids in air circulation.

12. The next morning, the first

Many breeders paper train their litters so that the house-breaking process is already underway when the puppies go to their new homes.

thing you do is take your dog out. The circle continues and the dog will learn.

Time, effort, consistency, praise...you are the key to effectively training your Dachshund puppy.

What Do You Do When You Catch Your Dog in the Act?

This is highly controversial. Spanking is not encouraged anywhere. I use words like "shame, bad dog." Then be sure to take the dog out. Dachshunds want to please you and letting them know they aren't doing that does get across to them.

Believe me, your dog can be housebroken but it takes consistency, diligence and love. Your dog must want to please you and understand the request and then it will happen.

You Can Teach Your Dog to Ask to Go Out

It should be fun to go out. Before you take a dog of any age out, stand in front of the door and do the happy recital of "Do you want to go out?" Let your dog jump up or circle, whatever he does naturally. Let him know you are pleased with his response. Do this with consistency. Use the same happy words that are usually based on going out.

Hopefully, after a while, the dog will jump up and down near the door or circle or bark or whatever you have taught him to say to let you know that he wants to go out.

Is Any One Variety or Size Harder to Housebreak?

There are different opinions on this topic. Longhairs seem to take best to going out in all elements. Smooths obviously dislike bad weather. Wires combine the blood of terriers who many say are hard to housebreak. Other people tell you miniatures are like toys and they are hard to train. I have also heard more longhairs discussed as being dirty dogs than any other variety.

I firmly believe that all types and varieties can be successfully housebroken even though many dogs are not. I believe you are the key.

TRAINING Your Dachshund

I n horses the most basic command is "back" to prove that the human is in control. With the smaller, more agile animal, the dog, the most needed command is "come." Come is an expression of love and it also proves who is in control. If you make it pleasurable to come, you will reap the benefits. In your lifetime with this dog, you may call him several thousand times.

When I trained a deaf dog, I learned how important body language is to animals. Children frighten dogs when they lean over them and wonder what they are doing. If you explain to a child that they are threatening the dog because they are approaching him like a menacing animal they understand better.

Basic obedience training is a necessity for your new friend, not just to teach him acceptable behavior but to keep him safe as well.

With deaf training, I learned that by getting down on my knees and opening my arms in an open hug-like gesture almost any animal, other than a completely wild one, will come to you. As a further extension of this theory, I explain to children that this is why an open palm held below a dog's nose with an outstretched arm is a friendly, welcoming gesture to a dog. First he can smell your scent and then he can come closer and get to know you.

With every new puppy, I start the training with the open arm gesture and "puppy name, come." Of course, I use the lyrical, happy voice used by dog lovers everywhere.

Ninety percent or so will learn with this gesture alone. Others are more stubborn or reserved. Sometimes, I put a young dog on a long lead and then I sit on the ground. I let him wander freely and then I call, "puppy come."

If they don't come immediately, I will pull the lead and repeat the call. Once they get there, I give hugs, love, kisses and, only from time to time, treats.

We all hope we won't need to be sure that our dog will come when called, but our contemporary lifestyle almost assures us that at some time this will be a need so do your training early.

I have had problems with cocky young dogs during puberty (selective deafness is a characteristic of many Dachshunds and when this melds with hunting or amour you may be in trouble). Our only defense against these problems is to try to be sure that our dogs will come when called. Puberty creates other temporary masters. Your only other defense is to keep your dog only in a fenced area or on a leash at all times.

Even when you do this there is always the time a dog pushes past a child at a door or the gardener leaves the gate open. On that day, no training of your dog will be more important. "Puppy come" is then the difference between life and death.

"Come" is one of the most basic, yet most important, commands you can teach your Dachshund. Successful practice is rewarded with a treat.

WALKING ON A LEASH

1. Before you start, put a thin nylon choke collar on your dog. Hold it in your left hand so the free end will be the base of a "P." When you put it on correctly, the end will pull from the left over the neck to where you will attach the lead. You are on the right of the dog. Then when the dog is on the left of you, and you jerk the collar, it releases immediately and never snags in a position that can gag the puppy. A standard puppy will probably wear a 12-inch choke collar; an older puppy a 14-inch and a few male adults a 16-inch.

2. Now attach your inch-wide six-foot lead with the smallest hook catch you can find to the puppy's collar. Remember to regularly adjust the collar to keep it as high on the neck as possible. Avoid letting it slip down to the middle or base of the neck, as this will panic and gag a puppy. (Try the positions on yourself and see what

One Dachshund on a leash is plenty to keep you on your toes—Catherine Carson has her hands full with five!

happens when you hold a hand on the highest point of your neck, in the middle and at the base. Once you see the difference on how it feels, you'll constantly be adjusting your puppy's collar and moving it up.)

3. Puppies hate to go through doors. So, on the first time out, I pick them up and carry them out to the closest grassy area. This way if they balk, refuse to go or turn into a bucking bronco, they won't be hurt in a doorway or on cement or blacktop.

4. If you have an older dog and a puppy, walk the two together. Puppies will follow another dog immediately. Keep you pocket full of puppy food or biscuits. Encourage him with "puppy come" commands, rewards and happy talk.

5. Don't take your puppy out on busy streets in the beginning stages of training. Try nice, quiet areas so he

can get used to the idea of being under your control. Let him hear the sounds of nature that will alert his hunting instincts. Don't burden his training with the frightening sounds of traffic that could, at this stage, affect his love of walking anywhere.

6. Don't exhaust your new puppy. In all things, animals learn for about 20 minutes. After that you are simply tiring them. When you get home, you can try encouraging your Dachshund to go through the door. If he doesn't, don't take a chance of the door hitting him. Either gently lead him through with food enticement or just pick him up if he resists. If you live where there are elevators, again pick him up and avoid his walking until he is more familiar with all the sounds and activity.

Puppies are full of energy, but they need time to rest, too. Keep this in mind when training your Dachshund and don't overwhelm him with too much too soon.

TRAIN YOUR PUPPY TO RIDE IN THE CAR

Here's another use for your trusty crate. We're going to make it fun for your pet to travel with you.

Don't feed him before you take him for rides. Talk to him while he is in the crate. If he cries, speak reassuringly. Take him somewhere he can play and have fun, like a park. Meet another friend with a friendly dog. You don't want his only memories of travel to be to a veterinarian or a kennel.

When you travel in a car with a dog, remember to leave windows open when your dog is crated. If the weather is hot, leave windows wide open as it will be hotter in the crate than it is in the rest of the car. Otherwise, if your dog is loose in a warm car, open all four windows so there is an air flow but don't open them so far that the dog could get out. And don't leave a dog alone in a car for more than 5-10

Riding in the car should be a fun experience for your Dachshund. A sturdy fiberglass crate will ensure his safety and prevent him from distracting the driver.

minutes without checking on him.

Most importantly, a dog can die within minutes in a very hot car with no air. Secondly, we know a famous Dachshund who ate a mink coat and the interior of a BMW while left free inside.

PROTECTING YOUR DACHSHUND'S BACK

Dachshunds have vulnerable backs. They are long dogs and their backs can be hurt terribly which can cripple them for life. Most, or at least many of these, disc injuries are accidents that could be avoided.

These accidents happen because dogs jump too vigorously from one surface to another, bound up or down stairs or race around corners at breakneck speed. This last bad habit is perhaps the worst culprit. Whenever you see the rear legs slipping out to the side on a dog racing around a corner, firmly tell him no. Make him stop and think about what he is doing.

If your voice isn't authoritative enough to stop him, put on a leash next time and jerk him to a stop and tell him no. Most dogs get in a habit of racing when they go out. Train against it and this may do more to prolong his life than anything else you read in this book.

If you can avoid slippery floor surfaces, like glossy tile, this also helps. And when you think of slick surfaces, remember a Dachshund can get hurt as much on ice and snow as you.

If you have stairs, don't let your dog go up and down more than once a day. Block the stairs off. If he persists in having trouble with stairs, then I'd suggest you just carry him up and down whenever it is necessary.

A Dachshund's long back makes him vulnerable to possible

The Dachshund's most distinctive, yet most vulnerable, feature is his long back. Climbing stairs, running fast, and being overweight are all causes of strain and possible injury.

injury. If you protect him from accidents, you will probably control the problem. Keeping your dog slim, but not skinny, will also aid this cause dramatically. Excess weight puts excess strain on the dog. With a Dachshund, a slim dog is a healthy dog.

Dachshunds don't have many of the problems of other breeds. They are not affected by hip dysplasia and many other genetic problems. What Dachshunds have are vulnerable backs. A little training and care will help you keep this from ever becoming a problem as well.

Sioux's Milky Way and Sioux's Baby Ruth, owned by Sue McClelland, are learning the value of quiet time.

The Dachshund is prone to certain types of injuries due to his unique body structure. Ch. Bermarg's Shoney of Boondox L is a picture-perfect example of the Dachshund body.

GROOMING the Dachshund

Dachshunds try to keep themselves clean and will frequently wash themselves like cats. If you follow these basic grooming needs, that's all you'll need to do. Although the Dachshund is a relatively easy breed to groom, you will have to keep up with basic maintenance so that your Dachshund stays clean and looking his best. Every Dachshund should be bathed every two to six weeks depending on his lifestyle. A dog who appears regularly in the show ring is usually bathed before each show weekend. The more frequent the baths, the more you are encouraging him to grow more hair and have a healthy coat. Any good pet shampoo will do the job. If you follow with a cream rinse, his hair and skin will

Dachshunds, especially Smooths, require relatively little grooming. However, regular baths are important to keep your Dachshund's skin and coat clean and healthy.

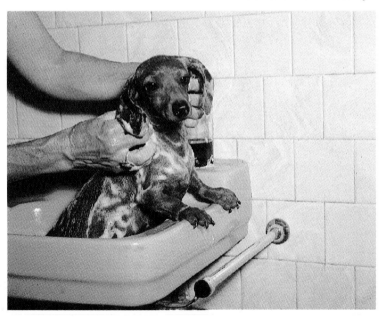

This lucky 12-week-old Dachshund pup has his own private bathtub.

benefit just as much as a human's.

Flea shampoos should only be used on puppies over 12 weeks (or whatever the label suggests). They never should be used more than once a week. These shampoos frequently stun the fleas. The physical movement of washing the dog removes them from the skin and sends them down the drain. Following with a flea dip gives the coat resistance against fleas who may try to jump "on board" during the next week or so. Read all directions carefully in mixing these dips as they are poisons. If they kill fleas, they can also harm your dog if you mix them too strong, use them too often, or if your dog has an allergic reaction to them.

Nails should be trimmed every other week. Long nails make a dog walk on the wrong parts of his feet and will hinder his balance. If he walks on cement regularly, you'll need to take off a lot less than a dog who spends his time in a grassy backyard.

The first trick of cutting nails is to get the dog comfortable. Some people cradle a dog in their laps and wrap their arms around him to confine him.

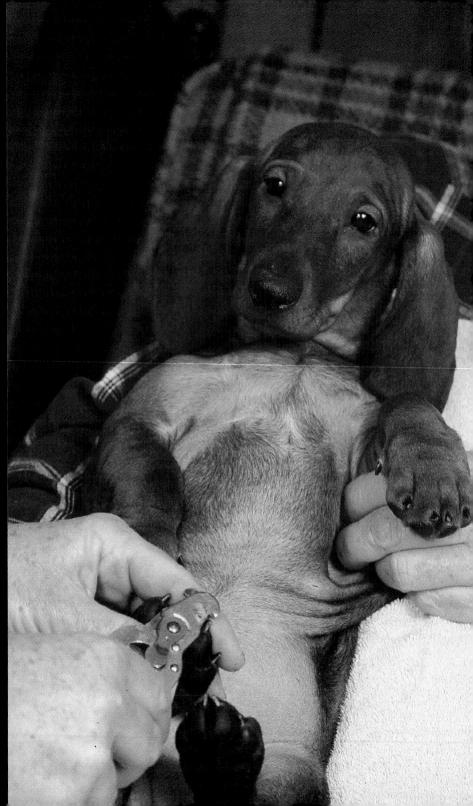

Once you've done this, start with the hind feet. They are the hardest to do. Do not use pressure with your hand in holding the foot. Death grips by novice owners will frighten dogs and make them shy of nail cutting.

Start nipping off the tips about ⅛ of an inch. As long as you see the white cuticle, you have cut a safe distance. If the nail starts to bleed, you have gone too far and cut the quick. There are styptic pencils and powders that you press the nail into to stop this bleeding. If you don't have them, you can use corn starch. And if you don't have that, simply use finger pressure, both on the top of the nail base and the end of the nail. You may feel quite guilty about "quicking" your puppy, but no puppy dies from a bleeding toenail. Simply try not to do it again.

Brushing and bathing is about all that is necessary for the pet Smooth; the show dog may require some clipping and a bit of coat oil for shine.

Once you've finished the back feet, do the front feet. If you do cut the nails regularly, every week or two, you'll never need to take off more than ⅛ to ⅓ of an inch. When you're done, praise your puppy and deliver some good treats or hugs. No dog likes having his nails cut, so you might as well make it as pleasant as possible.

Smooth Grooming

There is no easier variety to groom than the smooth Dachshund. Smooth Dachshunds are the epitome of the simple, spit-shine kind of dog.

Acclimating your Dachshund to the nail clipping routine at an early age and making him comfortable during the process will help make it a more pleasant experience for you both.

There is a mitt available with brush bristles sewn into the palm, called a "hound mitt." It is an excellent way to brush your dog's coat and help stimulate the skin's natural lubrication.

If you can't get a hound mitt, a soft bristle brush will do the same job almost as well. At shows, to give a dog a rich luster, spray a tiny amount of mink oil on the hound mitt and brush-massage it into the coat.

If your dog flakes dandruff, his skin is dry and needs some lubrication. Go to your local pet store and find a product that will help the skin slough off the dandruff layer and rebuild itself. A tablespoon of corn oil or vegetable oil in a dog's food will also help solve this problem, or there are oral supplements sold for this purpose. More frequent bathing will also help rectify this problem, as will following with a cream rinse.

When I show dogs, I snip off their whiskers and eyebrows. I do this to make the shape and line of the heads stand out more. Don't attempt this if you have an unsteady hand. Attempt it only if you have a blunt end and/or curved scissors. If you have any questions about being able to do this, visit the groomers in your area. Find one who knows how to trim show dogs.

Vibrant colors and a rich sheen give the smooth Dachshund's coat its simple beauty.

I also thin the seams on my showdogs. These are the areas up the front of the neck and up the rear where the hair comes together to form a cowlick seam. I use very short extra-fine thinning scissors. I cut from the bottom up and move toward where the hair grows. You do not want to see a line of demarcation. You only want to smooth and refine the natural seam. Again, if you have the slightest question about this, go to a good groomer. If your scissors aren't fine enough, your dog will be out of competition for weeks while he regrows hair.

LONGHAIR GROOMING

No one wins more in the longhair ring than Lorene Hogan. For the last several years she has shown three (that I

The longhaired Dachshund will require a little more maintenance to keep him looking his best, especially if he is a show dog.

remember) different dogs to the #1 title. She amasses Best in Show honors on a regular basis. All the dogs that Lorene shows are exquisitely groomed. She has consented to share some of her secrets with you and your groomer. As a novice in these areas, I'd like to alert you to a few basic problems. If you don't know what you are doing, go by the old adage, less is more. If you overthin a dog's coat on his back and the back of his neck, it can become curly and this curl can last for a lifetime. And as Lorene says, "Remember, cut, brush, look. You can't put it back on." (And it takes nature a couple of months to replace your mistake.)

Head

Looking down on your dog, and starting from the middle of the top of the dog's head, place your thinning shears (with the teeth on the top) close to the middle of the head. Begin to thin, from the back toward the nose. With the shears close to

Once they get used to it, many dogs grow to like being brushed. Aside from keeping the coat tangle-free, brushing also stimulates the dog's skin.

the skull to allow the cutting of undercoat, cut once, brush, then continue down to the side of the eye. Repeat until the desired look is achieved. Once you are satisfied with the results, start on the other side. Remember to keep the thinning shears with the teeth up and always brush after each cut.

To groom the ear, muzzle and cheek area, begin in the front of the ear with the shear's teeth closest to the ear. Cut in short rapid strokes, blending into the muzzle. Repeat if necessary, always brushing after each cut or series of cuts. Repeat on the other side.

Lift and hold the ear out of your way and thin underneath with straight scissors. You can use a stripping knife to remove the short fuzziness by combing it with the stripping knife.

Neck and Body

Have the shears with the teeth next to the ear of the dog. Cut at an angle down the side of the neck. Blending into the shoulders continue to the middle of the neck then turn your scissors over and repeat on the other side. Take small cuts in this area. On the back of the neck, your scissors should be placed vertical with the neck.

The throat should be cleaned out under the chin and side of the throat using the quick short cuts as used when you did the side of the head but much closer. I prefer not to go lower than the shoulder when cleaning out the front. At the top of your bib, shape an inverted V. With the scissors vertical, the teeth next to the center of the chest, thin to shape the front. Have someone move your dog, and watch him coming at you. Thin the front if needed and the wings on the side of the front legs if they are sticking out. On extremely heavy coated dogs do the same to the side of the body, on the pants, and the tail. On the tail, have your scissors with the teeth at the top, and cut at an angle.

In longer-coated dogs, there is always the chance of matting. Regular brushing can prevent this from becoming a problem for your Longhair.

Feet
Use the thinning shears to clean the puffy part by pulling the hair up between the toes. Clean the pads with straight scissors. On the back legs, comb the hair up and use thinning shears to even.

Equipment
1. Harpner Real Knife
2. Small thinning scissors
3. Straight scissors
4. Nail clippers
5. Small flexible toothbrush
6. Sense of humor and patience

I would recommend that you practice on a dog that you're not showing.

Remember, cut, brush, look. You cannot put it back on!

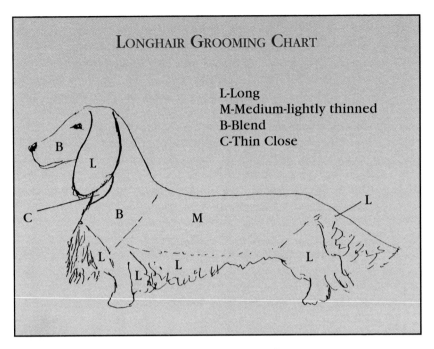

LONGHAIR GROOMING CHART

L-Long
M-Medium-lightly thinned
B-Blend
C-Thin Close

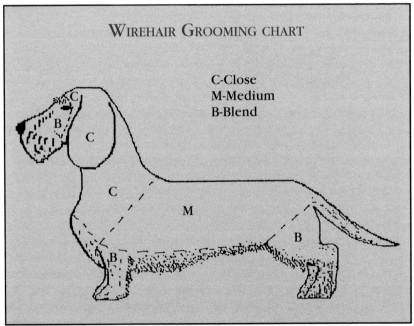

WIREHAIR GROOMING CHART

C-Close
M-Medium
B-Blend

I am no expert in grooming so I asked people to help me with these sections. Lynn Cope is a gregarious North Carolinian who breeds and shows her own Jeric Wirehair Dachshunds to top show awards including Best of Breed at the Dachshund Club of America National Specialty in 1992 with Ch. Jeric's Angel. As a groomer and kennel owner, she is the expert's expert when it comes to wirehairs.

Stripping

Terrier stripping is an art in itself. You will work with your thumb and index finger putting a lock of hair between the two. Roll your thumb up and around your index finger putting a minimal amount of pressure against the skin. The hair, which comes out easily this way, is now thrown away and the lock is stripped. Keep doing this, you have the entire dog to do.

Stripping should be done six to eight weeks before a show for the best look possible. Again strip the neck and head two to three weeks before a show and remove all dead hair from the ears regularly so they are smooth. Do not strip out the beard or brows. These are precious to those who appreciate all the charms of the wirehaired Dachshund.

Pet Grooming

Though we don't use clippers on show dogs, they can give a good effect on pets and simplify the grooming process for someone who doesn't know how to strip, have the hours necessary to do it or have the specialized skill needed for this variety.

Use a #10 blade for the close areas on the head and neck. You may need to pull hair from inside the ear canal. Shape the beard from the outside corner of the eye to the corner of the mouth and part and shape the eyebrows with thinning shears. (For show dogs, use a stripping knife.) Use a #9 or #7 blade for the medium length body hair.

Lynn also suggests you use a flea comb of a fine teeth style for daily combing. She tells me she has found that this will keep the head hair from building up in the coat and minimize shedding. She says it also keeps a pet looking like a show dog far longer than a grooming every eight weeks.

SPORT of Purebred Dogs

Welcome to the exciting and sometimes frustrating sport of dogs. No doubt you are trying to learn more about dogs or you wouldn't be deep into this book. This section covers the basics that may entice you, further your knowledge and help you to understand the dog world. If you decide to give showing, obedience or any other dog activities a try, then I suggest you seek further help from the appropriate source.

Dog showing has been a very popular sport for a long time and has been taken quite seriously by some. Others only enjoy it as a hobby.

The Kennel Club in England was formed in 1859, the American Kennel Club was established in 1884 and the Canadian Kennel Club was formed in 1888. The purpose of these clubs was to register purebred dogs and maintain their Stud Books. In the beginning, the concept of registering dogs was not readily accepted. More than 36 million dogs have been enrolled in the AKC Stud Book since its inception in 1888. Presently the kennel clubs not only register dogs but adopt and enforce rules and regulations governing dog shows, obedience trials and field trials. Over the years they have fostered and encouraged interest in the health and welfare of the purebred dog. They routinely donate funds to veterinary research for study on genetic disorders.

Below are the addresses of the kennel clubs in the United States, Great Britain and Canada.

The American Kennel Club
51 Madison Avenue
New York, NY 10010
(Their registry is located at: 5580 Centerview Drive, STE 200, Raleigh, NC 27606-3390)

The Kennel Club
1 Clarges Street

Piccadilly, London, WIY 8AB, England

The Canadian Kennel Club
111 Eglinton Avenue
East Toronto, Ontario M6S 4V7
Canada

Today there are numerous activities that are enjoyable for both the dog and the handler. Some of the activities include conformation showing, obedience competition, tracking, agility, the Canine Good Citizen Certificate, and a wide range of instinct tests that vary from breed to breed. Where you start depends upon your goals which early on may not be readily apparent.

At eight weeks old, future champion Siddach's Fiore already has elite taste. He thinks that this trophy, given by the Knickerbocker Dachshund Club, is a good place to hang out.

PUPPY KINDERGARTEN

Every puppy will benefit from this class. PKT is the foundation for all

future dog activities from conformation to "couch potatoes." Pet owners should make an effort to attend even if they never expect to show their dog. The class is designed for puppies about three months of age with graduation at approximately five months of age. All the puppies will be in the same age group and, even though some may be a little unruly, there should not be any real problem. This class will teach the puppy some beginning obedience. As in all obedience classes the owner learns how to train his own dog. The PKT class gives the puppy the opportunity to interact with other puppies in the same age group and exposes him to strangers, which is very important. Some dogs grow up with behavior problems, one of them being fear of strangers. As you can see, there can be much to gain from this class.

There are some basic obedience exercises that every dog should learn. Some of these can be started with puppy kindergarten.

Sit

One way of teaching the sit is to have your dog on your left side with the leash in your right hand, close to the collar. Pull up on the leash and at the same time reach around his hindlegs with your left hand and tuck them in. As you are doing this say, "Beau, sit." Always use the dog's name when you give an active command. Some owners like to use a treat holding it over the dog's head. The dog will need to sit to get the treat. Encourage the dog to hold the sit for a few seconds, which will eventually be the beginning of the Sit/Stay. Depending on how cooperative he is, you can rub him under the chin or stroke his back. It is a good time to establish eye contact.

Down

Sit the dog on your left side and kneel down beside him

Even a "couch potato" like seven-week-old Laddland Tea or Me will benefit from puppy kindergarten classes.

One day PKT, the next...who knows? This puppy grew up to be Ch. Geordach Simple Life and was Winners Dog at a Dachshund Club of America National Specialty.

with the leash in your right hand. Reach over him with your left hand and grasp his left foreleg. With your right hand, take his right foreleg and pull his legs forward while you say, "Beau, down." If he tries to get up, lean on his shoulder to encourage him to stay down. It will relax your dog if you stroke his back while he is down. Try to encourage him to stay down for a few seconds as preparation for the Down/Stay.

Heel

The definition of heeling is the dog walking under control at your left heel. Your puppy will learn controlled walking in the puppy kindergarten class, which will eventually lead to heeling. The command is "Beau, heel," and you start off briskly with your left foot. Your leash is in your right hand and your left hand is holding it about half way down. Your left hand should be able to control the leash and there should be a little slack in it. You want him to walk with you with your leg somewhere between his nose and his shoulder. You need to encourage him to stay with you, not forging (in front of you) or lagging behind you. It is best to keep him on a fairly short lead. Do not allow the lead to become tight. It is far better to give him a little jerk when necessary and remind him to heel. When you come to a halt, be prepared physically to make him sit. It takes practice to become coordinated. There are excellent books on training that you may wish to purchase. Your instructor should be able to recommend one for you.

Recall

This quite possibly is the most important exercise you will ever teach. It should be a pleasant experience. The puppy may learn to do random recalls while being attached to a long line such as a clothes line. Later the exercise will start with the dog sitting and staying until called. The command is "Beau, come." Let your command be happy.

In her day, Ch. Legibach's Ruby Slippers was one of the top-winning Wirehairs. She is shown here winning Best in Sweepstakes at the 1991 DCA Specialty.

You want your dog to come willingly and faithfully. The recall could save his life if he sneaks out the door. In practicing the recall, let him jump on you or touch you before you reach for him. If he is shy, then kneel down to his level. Reaching for the insecure dog could frighten him, and he may not be willing to come again in the future. Lots of praise and a treat would be in order whenever you do a recall. Under no circumstances should you ever correct your dog when he has come to you. Later in formal obedience your dog will be required to sit in front of you after recalling and then go to heel position.

CONFORMATION

Conformation showing is our oldest dog show sport. This type of showing is based on the dog's appearance–that is his structure, movement and attitude. When considering this type of showing, you need to be aware of your

Spanish Ch. Laddland Fashionably Late is an elegant smooth Dachshund. She has won several National Specialties and multiple international Bests in Show.

breed's standard and be able to evaluate your dog compared to that standard. The breeder of your puppy or other experienced breeders would be good sources for such an evaluation. Puppies can go through lots of changes over a period of time. I always say most puppies start out as promising hopefuls and then after maturing may be disappointing as show candidates. Even so this should not deter them from being excellent pets.

Usually conformation training classes are offered by the local kennel or obedience clubs. These are excellent places for training puppies. The puppy should be able to walk on a lead before entering such a class. Proper ring procedure and technique for posing (stacking) the dog will be demonstrated as well as gaiting the dog. Usually certain patterns are used in the ring such as the triangle or the "L." Conformation class, like the PKT class, will give your youngster the opportunity to socialize with different breeds of dogs and humans too.

It takes some time to learn the routine of conformation showing. Usually one starts at the puppy matches which may be AKC Sanctioned or Fun Matches. These matches are generally for puppies from two or three months to a year old, and there may be classes for the adult over the age of 12 months. Similar to point shows, the classes are divided by sex and after completion of the classes in that breed or variety, the class winners compete for Best of Breed or Variety. The winner goes on to compete in the Group and the Group winners compete for Best in Match. No championship points are awarded for match wins.

A few matches can be great training for puppies even though there is no intention to go on showing. Matches enable the puppy to meet new people and be handled by a stranger—the judge. It is also a change of environment, which broadens the horizon for both dog and handler. Matches and other dog activities boost the confidence of the handler and especially the younger handlers.

Earning an AKC championship is built on a point system, which is different from Great Britain. To become an AKC Champion of Record the dog must earn 15 points. The number of points earned each time depends upon the number of dogs in competition. The number of points available at each show depends upon the breed, its sex and the location of the show. The United States is divided into ten AKC zones. Each zone has its own set of points. The purpose of the zones is to try to equalize the points available from breed to breed and area to area.The AKC adjusts the point scale annually.

The number of points that can be won at a show are between one and five. Three-, four- and five-point wins are considered majors. Not only does the dog need 15 points won under three different judges, but those points must include two majors under two different judges. Canada also works on a point system but majors are not required.

Dogs always show before bitches. The classes available to those seeking points are: Puppy (which may be divided into 6 to 9 months and 9 to 12 months); 12 to 18 months; Novice; Bred-by-Exhibitor; American-bred; and Open. The class winners of the same sex of each breed or variety compete against each other for Winners Dog and Winners Bitch. A Reserve Winners Dog and Reserve Winners Bitch are also awarded but do not carry any points unless the Winners win is disallowed by AKC. The Winners Dog and Bitch compete with the specials (those dogs that have attained championship) for

Best of Breed or Variety, Best of Winners and Best of Opposite Sex. It is possible to pick up an extra point or even a major if the points are higher for the defeated winner than those of Best of Winners. The latter would get the higher total from the defeated winner.

At an all-breed show, each Best of Breed or Variety winner will go on to his respective Group and then the Group winners will compete against each other for Best in Show. There are seven Groups: Sporting, Hounds, Working, Terriers, Toys, Non-Sporting and Herding. Obviously there are no Groups at speciality shows (those shows that have only one breed or a show such as the American Spaniel Club's Flushing Spaniel Show, which is for all flushing spaniel breeds).

Catherine Carson and Scarlett get an early start on a field trial. In England, a dog must qualify in a working capacity as well as in conformation in order to become a champion.

Earning a championship in England is somewhat different since they do not have a point system. Challenge Certificates are awarded if the judge feels the dog is deserving regardless of the number of dogs in competition. A dog must earn three Challenge Certificates under three different judges, with at least one of these Certificates being won after the age of 12 months. Competition is very strong and entries may be higher than they are in the U.S. The Kennel Club's Challenge Certificates are only available at Championship Shows.

In England, The Kennel Club regulations require that certain dogs, Border Collies and Gundog breeds, qualify in a working capacity (i.e., obedience or field trials) before becoming a full Champion. If they do not qualify in the working aspect, then they are designated a Show Champion, which is equivalent to the AKC's Champion of Record. A Gundog may be granted the title of Field Trial Champion (FT Ch.) if it passes all the tests in the field but would also have to qualify in conformation before becoming a full Champion. A Border Collie that earns the title of Obedience Champion (Ob Ch.) must also qualify in the conformation ring before becoming a Champion.

The U.S. doesn't have a designation full Champion but does award for Dual and Triple Champions. The Dual Champion must be a Champion of Record, and either Champion Tracker, Herding Champion, Obedience Trial Champion or Field Champion. Any dog that has been awarded the titles of Champion of Record, and any two of the following: Champion Tracker, Herding Champion, Obedience Trial Champion or Field Champion, may be designated as a Triple Champion.

The shows in England seem to put more emphasis on breeder judges than those in the U.S. There is much competition within the breeds. Therefore the quality of the individual breeds should be very good. In the United States we tend to have more "all around judges" (those that judge multiple breeds) and use the breeder judges at the specialty shows. Breeder judges are more familiar with their own breed since they are actively breeding that breed or did so at one time. Americans emphasize Group and Best in Show wins and promote them accordingly.

It is my understanding that the shows in England can be very large and extend over several days, with the Groups being scheduled on different days. I believe there is only one all-breed show in the U.S. that extends over two days, the Westminster Kennel Club Show. In our country we have cluster shows, where several different clubs will use the same show site over consecutive days.

Westminster Kennel Club is our most prestigious show although the entry is limited to 2500. In recent years, entry has

The Westminster Kennel Club dog show is the most prestigious show in the United States. It is held annually at Madison Square Garden in New York City.

been limited to Champions. This show is more formal than the majority of the shows with the judges wearing formal attire and the handlers fashionably dressed. In most instances the quality of the dogs is superb. After all, it is a show of Champions. It is a good show to study the AKC registered breeds and is by far the most exciting—especially since it is televised! WKC is one of the few shows in this country that is still benched. This means the dog must be in his benched area during the show hours except when he is being groomed, in the ring, or being exercised.

A thin show lead, like the one this Dachshund is wearing, is commonly used to present a dog in the show ring.

Typically, the handlers are very particular about their appearances. They are careful not to wear something that will detract from their dog but will perhaps enhance it. American ring procedure is quite formal compared to that of other countries. I remember being reprimanded by a judge because I made a suggestion to a friend holding my second dog outside the ring. I certainly could have used more discretion so I would not call attention to myself. There is a certain etiquette expected between the judge and exhibitor and among the other exhibitors. Of course it is not always the case but the judge is supposed to be polite, not engaging in small talk or even acknowledging that he knows the handler. I understand that there is a more informal and relaxed atmosphere at the shows in other countries. For instance, the dress code is more casual. I can see where this might be more fun for the exhibitor and especially for the novice. This country is very handler-oriented in many of the breeds. It is true, in most instances, that the experienced professional handler can present the dog better and will have a feel for what a judge likes.

In England, Crufts is The Kennel Club's own show and is most assuredly the largest dog show in the world. They've been known to have an entry of nearly 20,000, and the show lasts four days. Entry is only gained by qualifying through winning in specified classes at another Championship Show.

Westminster is strictly conformation, but Crufts exhibitors and spectators enjoy not only conformation but obedience, agility and a multitude of exhibitions as well. Obedience was admitted in 1957 and agility in 1983.

If you are handling your own dog, please give some consideration to your apparel. For sure the dress code at matches is more informal than the point shows. However, you should wear something a little more appropriate than beach attire or ragged jeans and bare feet. If you check out the handlers and see what is presently fashionable, you'll catch on. Men usually dress with a shirt and tie and a nice sports coat. Whether you are male or female, you will want to wear comfortable clothes and shoes. You need to be able to run with your dog and you certainly don't want to take a chance of falling and hurting yourself. Heaven forbid, if nothing else, you'll upset your dog. Women usually wear a dress or two-piece outfit, preferably with pockets to carry bait, comb, brush, etc. In this case men are the lucky ones with all their pockets. Ladies, think about where your dress will be if you need to kneel on the floor and also think about running. Does it allow freedom to do so?

Years ago, after toting around all the baby paraphernalia, I found toting the dog and necessities a breeze. You need to take along dog; crate; ex pen (if you use one); extra newspaper; water pail and water; all required grooming equipment, including hair dryer and extension cord; table; chair for you; bait for dog and lunch for you and friends; and, last but not least, clean up materials, such as plastic bags, paper towels, and perhaps a bath towel and some shampoo—just in case. Don't forget your entry confirmation and directions to the show.

If you are showing in obedience, then you will want to wear pants. Many of our top obedience handlers wear pants that are color-coordinated with their dogs. The philosophy is that imperfections in the black dog will be less obvious next to your black pants.

Whether you are showing in conformation or obedience, you need to watch the clock and be sure you are not late. It is customary to pick up your conformation armband a few minutes before the start of the class. They will not wait for you and if you are on the show grounds and not in the ring, you will upset everyone. It's a little more complicated picking up your obedience armband if you show later in the class. If you have not picked up your armband and they get to your number, you may not be allowed to show. It's best to pick up your armband early, but then you may show earlier than expected if other handlers don't pick up. Customarily all conflicts should be discussed with the judge prior to the start of the class.

CANINE GOOD CITIZEN

The AKC sponsors a program to encourage dog owners to train their dogs. Local clubs perform the pass/fail tests, and dogs who pass are awarded a Canine Good Citizen Certificate. Proof of vaccination is required at the time of participation. The test includes:

The true mark of a Canine Good Citizen is being able to get along with other dogs. Ch. Solong Squire v Bristleknoll and Ch. Bayard La Lucille rub noses.

1. Accepting a friendly stranger.
2. Sitting politely for petting.
3. Appearance and grooming.
4. Walking on a loose leash.
5. Walking through a crowd.

6. Sit and down on command/staying in place.

7. Come when called.

8. Reaction to another dog.

9. Reactions to distractions.

10. Supervised separation.

If more effort was made by pet owners to accomplish these exercises, fewer dogs would be cast off to the humane shelter.

Unusual friends, this longhaired Dachshund and Great Dane adore each other. If only all dogs could get along this well! Both dogs are owned by Lorraine Genieczko.

OBEDIENCE

Obedience is necessary, without a doubt, but it can also become a wonderful hobby or even an obsession. In my opinion, obedience classes and competition can provide wonderful companionship, not only with your dog but with your classmates or fellow competitors. It is always gratifying to discuss your dog's problems with others who have had similar experiences. The AKC acknowledged Obedience around 1936, and it has changed tremendously even though many of the exercises are basically the same. Today, obedience competition is just that—very competitive. Even so, it is possible for every obedience exhibitor to come home a winner (by earning qualifying scores) even though he/she may not earn a placement in the class.

Most of the obedience titles are awarded after earning three qualifying scores (legs) in the appropriate class under three different judges. These classes offer a perfect score of 200, which is extremely rare. Each of the class exercises has its own point value. A leg is earned after receiving a score of at least 170 and at least 50 percent of the points available in each exercise. The titles are:

Companion Dog—CD

This is called the Novice Class and the exercises are:

1. Heel on leash and figure 8	40 points
2. Stand for examination	30 points
3. Heel free	40 points
4. Recall	30 points
5. Long sit—one minute	30 points
6. Long down—three minutes	30 points
Maximum total score	200 points

Companion Dog Excellent—CDX
This is the Open Class and the exercises are:

1. Heel off leash and figure 8	40 points
2. Drop on recall	30 points
3. Retrieve on flat	20 points
4. Retrieve over high jump	30 points
5. Broad jump	20 points
6. Long sit—three minutes (out of sight)	30 points
7. Long down—five minutes (out of sight)	30 points
Maximum total score	200 points

Utility Dog—UD
The Utility Class exercises are:

1. Signal Exercise	40 points
2. Scent discrimination—Article 1	30 points
3. Scent discrimination—Article 2	30 points
4. Directed retrieve	30 points
5. Moving stand and examination	30 points
6. Directed jumping	40 points
Maximum total score	200 points

After achieving the UD title, you may feel inclined to go after the UDX and/or OTCh. The UDX (Utility Dog Excellent) title went into effect in January 1994. It is not easily attained. The title requires qualifying simultaneously ten times in Open B and Utility B but not necessarily at consecutive shows.

The OTCh (Obedience Trial Champion) is awarded after the dog has earned his UD and then goes on to earn 100 championship points, a first place in Utility, a first place in Open and another first place in either class. The placements must be won under three

Show puppies start their training at a very young age. Sioux's Movie Star, owned by Sue McClelland, learns to stand using a treat as a motivator.

Catherine Carson and four of her Twelfth Night Dachshunds at canine camp. Camps like this give dogs and owners an opportunity to experience many aspects of the dog sport.

different judges at all-breed obedience trials. The points are determined by the number of dogs competing in the Open B and Utility B classes. The OTCh title precedes the dog's name.

Obedience matches (AKC Sanctioned, Fun, and Show and Go) are usually available. Usually they are sponsored by the local obedience clubs. When preparing an obedience dog for a title, you will find matches very helpful. Fun Matches and Show and Go Matches are more lenient in allowing you to make corrections in the ring. I frequently train (correct) in the ring and inform the judge that I would like to do so and to please mark me "exhibition." This means that I will not be eligible for any prize. This type of training is usually very necessary for the Open and Utility Classes. AKC Sanctioned Obedience Matches do not allow corrections in the ring since they must abide by the AKC Obedience Regulations. If you are interested in showing in obedience, then you should contact the AKC for a copy of the Obedience Regulations.

TRACKING

Tracking is officially classified obedience, but I feel it should have its own category. There are three tracking titles available: Tracking Dog (TD), Tracking Dog Excellent (TDX), Variable Surface Tracking (VST). If all three tracking titles are obtained, then the dog officially becomes a CT (Champion Tracker). The CT will go in front of the dog's name.

A TD may be earned anytime and does not have to follow the other obedience titles. There are many exhibitors that prefer tracking to obedience, and there are others like myself that do both. In my experience with small dogs, I prefer to earn the CD and CDX before attempting tracking. My reasoning is that small dogs are closer to the mat in the obedience rings and therefore it's too easy to put the nose down and sniff. Tracking encourages sniffing. Of course this depends on the dog. I've had some dogs that tracked around the ring and others (TDXs) who wouldn't think of sniffing in the ring.

AGILITY

Agility was first introduced by John Varley in England at the Crufts Dog Show, February 1978, but Peter Meanwell, competitor and judge, actually developed the idea. It was officially recognized in the early '80s. Agility is extremely popular in England and Canada and growing in popularity in the U.S. The AKC acknowledged agility in August 1994. Dogs

Ch. Ivic's Advance Notice has earned many obedience and tracking titles. Wearing his tracking harness, he stops to indicate that he has found the glove at the end of the course.

must be at least 12 months of age to be entered. It is a fascinating sport that the dog, handler and spectators enjoy to the utmost. Agility is a spectator sport! The dog performs off lead. The handler either runs with his dog or positions himself on the course and directs his dog with verbal and hand signals over a timed course over or through a variety of obstacles including a time out or pause.

Agility is a relatively new, yet popular, dog sport that can best be described as an obstacle course for dogs. Rusty jumps through a tire on the agility course.

One of the reasons for agility's popularity is that it is fun for the dogs, handlers, and spectators. Rusty makes his way to the end of a tunnel.

One of the main drawbacks to agility is finding a place to train. The obstacles take up a lot of space and it is very time consuming to put up and take down courses.

The titles earned at AKC agility trials are Novice Agility Dog (NAD), Open Agility Dog (OAD), Agility Dog Excellent (ADX), and Master Agility Excellent (MAX). In order to acquire an agility title, a dog must earn a qualifying score in its respective class on three separate occasions under two different judges. The MAX will be awarded after earning ten qualifying scores in the Agility Excellent Class.

PERFORMANCE TESTS

During the last decade the American Kennel Club has promoted performance tests–those events that test the different breeds' natural abilities. This type of event encourages a handler to devote even more time to his dog and retain the natural instincts of his breed heritage. It is an important part of the wonderful world of dogs.

Earthdog Events

For small terriers (Australian, Bedlington, Border, Cairn, Dandie Dinmont, Fox (Smooth & Wire), Lakeland, Norfolk, Norwich, Scottish, Sealyham, Skye, Welsh, West Highland White and Dachshunds).

Limited registration (ILP) dogs are eligible and all entrants must be at least six months of age. The primary purpose of the small terriers and Dachshunds is to pursue quarry to ground, hold the game, and alert the hunter where to dig, or to bolt. There are two parts to the test: (1) the approach to the quarry and (2) working the quarry. The dog must pass both parts for a

Areas of competition like Earthdog tests evaluate a dog's natural abilities. Dachshunds and many of the terrier breeds are natural hunters and diggers.

Junior Earthdog (JE). The Senior Earthdog (SE) must do a third part–to leave the den on command. The Master Earthdog (ME) is a bit more complicated.
This information has been taken from the AKC Guidelines.

General Information

Obedience, tracking and agility allow the purebred dog with an Indefinite Listing Privilege (ILP) number or a limited registration to be exhibited and earn titles. Application must be made to the AKC for an ILP number.

Ch. Twelfth Night's Miss Scarlett and Ch. Twelfth Night's 'Xpress Rusty L sit atop the agility climbing tower.

The American Kennel Club publishes a monthly *Events* magazine that is part of the *Gazette*, their official journal for the sport of purebred dogs. The *Events* section lists upcoming shows and the secretary or superintendent for them. The majority of the conformation shows in the U.S. are overseen by licensed superintendents. Generally the entry closing date is approximately two-and-a-half weeks before the actual show. Point shows are fairly expensive, while the match shows cost about one third of the point show entry fee. Match shows usually take entries the day of the show but some are pre-entry. The best way to find match show information is through your local kennel club. Upon asking, the AKC can provide you with a list of superintendents, and you can write and ask to be put on their mailing lists.

Obedience trial and tracking test information is available through the AKC. Frequently these events are not superintended, but put on by the host club. Therefore you would make the entry with the event's secretary.

As you have read, there are numerous activities you can share with your dog. Regardless what you do, it does take teamwork. Your dog can only benefit from your attention and training. I hope this chapter has enlightened you and hope, if nothing else, you will attend a show here and there. Perhaps you will start with a puppy kindergarten class, and who knows where it may lead!

HEALTH CARE

Veterinary medicine has become far more sophisticated than what was available to our ancestors. This can be attributed to the increase in household pets and consequently the demand for better care for them. Also human medicine has become far more complex. Today diagnostic testing in veterinary medicine parallels human diagnostics. Because of better technology we can expect our pets to live healthier lives thereby increasing their life spans.

A healthy puppy is a happy puppy! Veterinary care should be your first priority when acquiring a new puppy. This is 11-week-old Laddland Audacious.

THE FIRST CHECK UP

You will want to take your new puppy/dog in for its first check up within 48 to 72 hours after acquiring it. Many breeders strongly recommend this check up and so do the humane shelters. A puppy/dog can appear healthy but it may have a serious problem that is not apparent to the layman. Most pets have some type of a minor flaw that may never cause a real problem.

Unfortunately if he/she should have a serious problem, you will want to consider the consequences of keeping the pet and the attachments that will be formed, which may be broken prematurely. Keep in mind there are many healthy dogs looking for good homes.

This first check up is a good time to establish yourself with the veterinarian and learn the office policy regarding their hours and how they handle emergencies. Usually the breeder or another conscientious pet owner is a good reference for locating a capable veterinarian. You should be aware that not all veterinarians give the same quality of service. Please do not make your selection on the least expensive clinic, as they may be short changing your pet. There is the possibility that eventually it will cost you more due to improper diagnosis, treatment, etc. If you are selecting a new veterinarian, feel free to ask for a tour of the clinic. You should inquire about making

an appointment for a tour since all clinics are working clinics, and therefore may not be available all day for sightseers. You may worry less if you see where your pet will be spending the day if he ever needs to be hospitalized.

THE PHYSICAL EXAM

Your veterinarian will check your pet's overall condition, which includes listening to the heart; checking the respiration; feeling the abdomen, muscles and joints; checking the mouth, which includes the gum color and signs of gum disease along with plaque buildup; checking the ears for signs of an infection or ear mites; examining the eyes; and, last but not least, checking the condition of the skin and coat.

Your Dachshund's physical exam will include a thorough examination of the mouth, teeth, and gums to detect any plaque or gum disease.

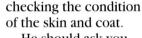

He should ask you questions regarding your pet's eating and elimination habits and invite you to relay your questions. It is a good idea to prepare a list so as not to forget anything. He should discuss the proper diet and the quantity to be fed. If this should differ from your breeder's recommendation, then you should

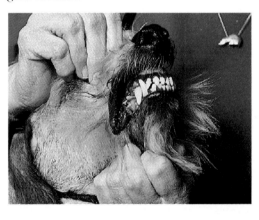

convey to him the breeder's choice and see if he approves. If he recommends changing the diet, then this should be done over a few days so as not to cause a gastrointestinal upset. It is customary to take in a fresh stool sample (just a small amount) for a test for intestinal parasites. It must be fresh, preferably within 12 hours, since the eggs hatch quickly and after hatching will not be observed under the microscope. If your pet isn't obliging then, usually the technician can take one in the clinic.

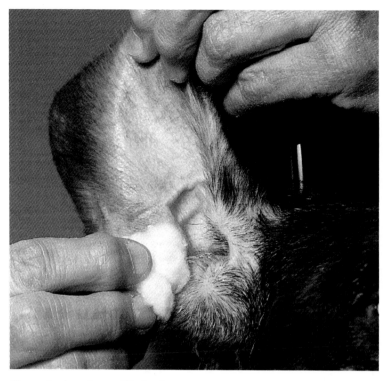

The veterinarian will check your Dachshund's ears during his physical, but it is up to you to keep up with regular cleaning and inspection at home.

IMMUNIZATIONS

It is important that you take your puppy/dog's vaccination record with you on your first visit. In case of a puppy, presumably the breeder has seen to the vaccinations up to the time you acquired custody. Veterinarians differ in their vaccination protocol. It is not unusual for your puppy to have received vaccinations for distemper, hepatitis, leptospirosis, parvovirus and parainfluenza every two to three weeks from the age of five or six weeks. Usually this is a combined injection and is typically called the DHLPP. The DHLPP is given through at least 12 to 14 weeks of age, and it is customary to continue with another parvovirus vaccine at 16 to 18 weeks. You may wonder why so many immunizations are necessary. No one knows for sure when the puppy's maternal antibodies are gone, although it is

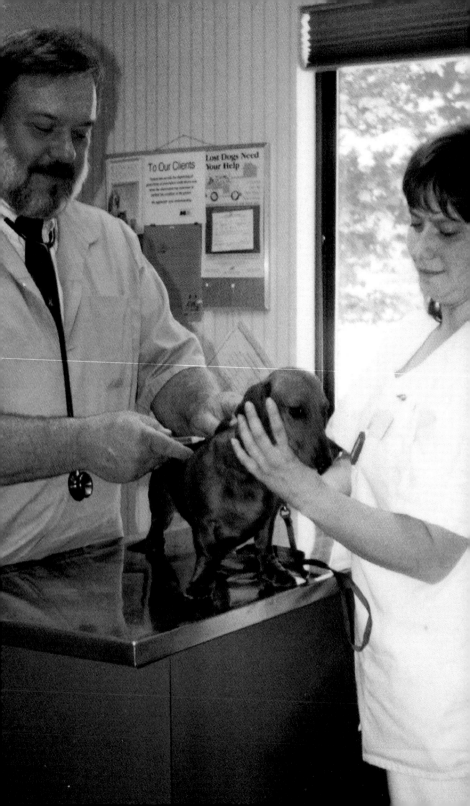

customarily accepted that distemper antibodies are gone by 12 weeks. Usually parvovirus antibodies are gone by 16 to 18 weeks of age. However, it is possible for the maternal antibodies to be gone at a much earlier age or even a later age. Therefore immunizations are started at an early age. The vaccine will not give immunity as long as there are maternal antibodies.

The rabies vaccination is given at three or six months of age depending on your local laws. A vaccine for bordetella (kennel cough) is advisable and can be given anytime from the age of five weeks. The coronavirus is not commonly given unless there is a problem locally. The Lyme vaccine is necessary in endemic areas. Lyme disease has been reported in 47 states.

An upcoming trip to the veterinarian can make some Dachshunds want to hide!

Distemper

This is virtually an incurable disease. If the dog recovers, he is subject to severe nervous disorders. The virus attacks every tissue in the body and resembles a bad cold with a fever. It can cause a runny nose and eyes and cause gastrointestinal disorders, including a poor appetite, vomiting and diarrhea. The virus is carried by raccoons, foxes, wolves, mink and other dogs. Unvaccinated youngsters and senior citizens are very susceptible. This is still a common disease.

Hepatitis

This is a virus that is most serious in very young dogs. It is spread by contact with an infected animal or its stool or urine. The virus affects the liver and kidneys and is characterized by high fever, depression and lack of appetite. Recovered animals may be afflicted with chronic illnesses.

A veterinary technician comforts a Dachshund puppy while he receives a vaccination.

Leptospirosis

This is a bacterial disease transmitted by contact with the urine of an infected dog, rat or other wildlife. It produces severe symptoms of fever, depression, jaundice and internal bleeding and was fatal before the vaccine was

Young puppies are particularly susceptible to certain diseases; the risk of transmitting disease increases when pups are kept together.

developed. Recovered dogs can be carriers, and the disease can be transmitted from dogs to humans.

Parvovirus

This was first noted in the late 1970s and is still a fatal disease. However, with proper vaccinations, early diagnosis and prompt treatment, it is a manageable disease. It attacks the bone marrow and intestinal tract. The symptoms include depression, loss of appetite, vomiting, diarrhea and collapse. Immediate medical attention is of the essence.

Rabies

This is shed in the saliva and is carried by raccoons, skunks, foxes, other dogs and cats. It attacks nerve tissue, resulting in paralysis and death. Rabies can be transmitted to people and is virtually always fatal. This disease is reappearing in the suburbs.

Bordetella (Kennel Cough)

The symptoms are coughing, sneezing, hacking and retching accompanied by nasal discharge usually lasting from a few days to several weeks. There are several disease-producing organisms responsible for this disease. The present vaccines are helpful but do not protect for all the strains. It usually is not life threatening but in some instances it can progress to a serious bronchopneumonia. The disease is highly contagious. The vaccination should be given routinely for dogs that come in contact with other dogs, such as through boarding, training class or visits to the groomer.

Coronavirus

This is usually self limiting and not life threatening. It was first noted in the late '70s about a year before parvovirus. The virus produces a yellow/brown stool and there may be depression, vomiting and diarrhea.

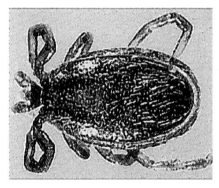

The deer tick is the most common carrier of Lyme disease. Photo courtesy of Virbac Laboratories, Inc., Fort Worth, Texas.

Lyme Disease

This was first diagnosed in the United States in 1976 in Lyme, CT in people who lived in close proximity to the deer tick. Symptoms may include acute lameness, fever, swelling of joints and loss of appetite. Your veterinarian can advise you if you live in an endemic area.

After your puppy has completed his puppy vaccinations, you will continue to booster the DHLPP once a year. It is customary to booster the rabies one year after the first vaccine and then, depending on where you live, it should be boostered every year or every three years. This depends on your local laws. The Lyme and corona vaccines are boostered annually and it is recommended that the bordetella be boostered every six to eight months.

ANNUAL VISIT

I would like to impress the importance of the annual check up, which would include the booster vaccinations, check for intestinal parasites and test for heartworm. Today in our very busy world it is rush, rush and see "how much you can get for how little." Unbelievably, some non-veterinary businesses have entered into the vaccination business. More harm than good can come to your dog through improper vaccinations, possibly from inferior vaccines and/or the wrong schedule. More than likely you truly care about your companion dog and over the years you have devoted much time and expense to his well being. Perhaps you are unaware that a vaccination is not just a vaccination. There is more involved. Please, please follow through with regular physical examinations. It is so important for your veterinarian to know your dog and this is especially

As your Dachshund matures, he will need to go to the veterinarian at least once a year for a check up. This Smooth visits Dr. Richard Smolen of Duncan Manor Animal Hospital.

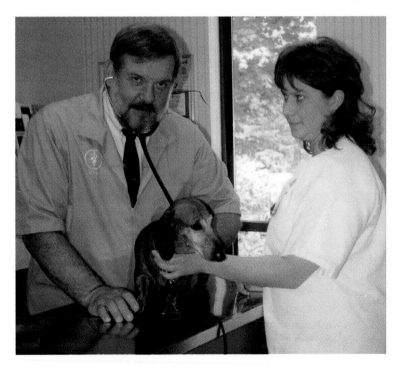

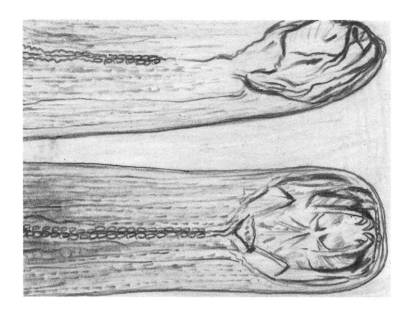

Hookworms are almost microscopic intestinal worms that can cause anemia and therefore serious problems, including death.

true during middle age through the geriatric years. More than likely your older dog will require more than one physical a year. The annual physical is good preventive medicine. Through early diagnosis and subsequent treatment your dog can maintain a longer and better quality of life.

INTESTINAL PARASITES

Hookworms

These are almost microscopic intestinal worms that can cause anemia and therefore serious problems, including death, in young puppies. Hookworms can be transmitted to humans through penetration of the skin. Puppies may be born with them.

Roundworms

These are spaghetti-like worms that can cause a potbellied appearance and dull coat along with more severe symptoms, such as vomiting, diarrhea and coughing. Puppies acquire these while in the mother's uterus and through lactation. Both hookworms and roundworms may be acquired through ingestion.

Whipworms

These have a three-month life cycle and are not acquired through the dam. They cause intermittent diarrhea usually with mucus. Whipworms are possibly the most difficult worm to eradicate. Their eggs are very resistant to most environmental factors and can last for years until the proper conditions enable them to mature. Whipworms are seldom seen in the stool.

Intestinal parasites are more prevalent in some areas than others. Climate, soil and contamination are big factors contributing to the incidence of intestinal parasites. Eggs are passed in the stool, lay on the ground and then become infective in a certain number of days. Each of the above

Whipworms are possibly the most difficult worm to eradicate. They cause intermittent diarrhea usually with mucus. Courtesy of Merck AgVet.

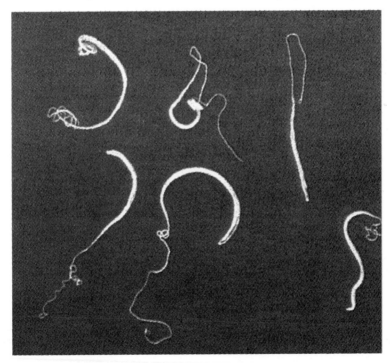

worms has a different life cycle. Your best chance of becoming and remaining worm-free is to always pooper-scoop your yard. A fenced-in yard keeps stray dogs out, which is certainly helpful.

I would recommend having a fecal examination on your dog twice a year or more often if there is a problem. If your dog has a positive fecal sample, then he will be given the appropriate medication and you will be asked to bring back another stool sample in a certain period of time (depending on the type of worm) and then be rewormed. This process goes on until he has at least two negative samples. The different types of worms require different medications. You will be wasting your money and doing your dog an injustice by buying over-the-counter medication without first consulting your veterinarian.

Puppies like to play with each other but, unfortunately, they can also pass along diseases and parasites. Proper vaccination is a must—it could save your dog's life!

OTHER INTERNAL PARASITES

Coccidiosis and Giardiasis

These protozoal infections usually affect puppies, especially in places where large numbers of puppies are brought together. Older dogs may harbor these infections but do not show signs unless they are stressed. Symptoms include diarrhea, weight loss and lack of appetite. These infections are not always apparent in the fecal examination.

Tapeworms

Seldom apparent on fecal floatation, they are diagnosed frequently as rice-like segments around the dog's anus and the base of the tail. Tapeworms are long, flat and ribbon like, sometimes several feet in length, and made up of many segments about five-eighths of an inch long. The two most common types of tapeworms found in the dog are:

(1) First the larval form of the flea tapeworm parasite must

mature in an intermediate host, the flea, before it can become infective. Your dog acquires this by ingesting the flea through licking and chewing.

(2) Rabbits, rodents and certain large game animals serve as intermediate hosts for other species of tapeworms. If your dog should eat one of these infected hosts, then he can acquire tapeworms.

HEARTWORM DISEASE

This is a worm that resides in the heart and adjacent blood vessels of the lung that produces microfilaria, which circulate in the bloodstream. It is possible for a dog to be infected with any number of worms from one to a hundred that can be 6 to 14 inches long. It is a life-threatening disease, expensive to treat and easily prevented. Depending on where you live, your veterinarian may recommend a preventive year-round and either an annual or semiannual blood test. The most common preventive is given once a month.

EXTERNAL PARASITES

Fleas

These pests are not only the dog's worst enemy but also enemy to the owner's pocketbook. Preventing is less expensive than treating, but regardless I think we'd prefer to spend our money elsewhere. I would guess that the majority of our dogs are allergic to the bite of a flea, and in many cases it only takes one flea bite. The protein in the flea's saliva is the culprit. Allergic dogs have a reaction, which usually results in a "hot spot." More than likely such a reaction will involve a trip to the veterinarian for treatment. Yes, prevention is less expensive. Fortunately today there are several good products available.

If there is a flea infestation, no one product is going to correct the problem. Not only will the dog require treatment so will the environment. In general flea collars are not very effective although there is now available an "egg" collar that will kill the eggs on the dog. Dips are the most economical but they are messy. There are some effective shampoos and treatments available through pet shops and veterinarians. An oral tablet arrived on the American market in 1995 and was popular in Europe the previous year. It sterilizes the female flea but will not kill adult fleas. Therefore the tablet, which is given monthly, will decrease the flea population but is not a "cure-all." Those dogs that suffer from flea-bite allergy will still be subjected to the bite of the flea. Another popular parasiticide is permethrin, which is applied to the back of the dog in one or two places depending on the dog's weight. This product works as a repellent causing the flea to get "hot feet" and jump off. Do not confuse this product with some of the organophosphates that are also applied to the dog's back.

Some products are not usable on young puppies. Treating fleas should be done under your veterinarian's guidance. Frequently it is necessary to combine products and the layman does not have the knowledge regarding possible toxicities. It is hard to believe but there are a few dogs that do have a natural resistance to fleas. Nevertheless it would be wise to treat all pets at the same time. Don't forget your cats. Cats just love to prowl the neighborhood and consequently return with unwanted guests.

To prevent and eliminate flea infestation, use a safe insecticide to kill adult fleas in the house and insect growth regulator to stop the eggs and larvae in the environment.

Adult fleas live on the dog but their eggs drop off the dog into the environment. There they go through four larval stages before reaching adulthood, and thereby are able to jump back on the poor unsuspecting dog. The cycle resumes and takes between 21 to 28 days under ideal conditions. There are environmental products available that will kill both the adult fleas and the larvae.

Ticks

Ticks carry Rocky Mountain Spotted Fever, Lyme disease and can cause tick paralysis. They should be removed with tweezers, trying to pull out the head. The jaws carry disease. There is a tick preventive collar that does an excellent job. The ticks automatically back out on those dogs wearing collars.

Sarcoptic Mange

This is a mite that is difficult to find on skin scrapings. The pinnal reflex is a good indicator of this disease. Rub the ends of the pinna (ear) together and the dog will start scratching with his foot. Sarcoptes are highly contagious to other dogs and to humans although they do not live long on humans. They cause intense itching.

Demodectic Mange

This is a mite that is passed from the dam to her puppies. It affects youngsters age three to ten months. Diagnosis is confirmed by skin scraping. Small areas of alopecia around the eyes, lips and/or forelegs become visible. There is little itching unless there is a secondary bacterial infection. Some breeds are afflicted more than others.

Dachshunds love to romp and play outside, which puts them at risk of picking up ticks. Be sure to thoroughly inspect your dog for ticks every time he comes in from outside.

Cheyletiella

This causes intense itching and is diagnosed by skin scraping. It lives in the outer layers of the skin of dogs, cats, rabbits and humans. Yellow-gray scales may be found on the back and the rump, top of the head and the nose.

All Dachshund puppies look cute but not all are of breeding quality. Breeders usually sell pet quality puppies with the requirement that the puppies are spayed or neutered.

TO BREED OR NOT TO BREED

More than likely your breeder has requested that you have your puppy neutered or spayed. Your breeder's request is based on what is healthiest for your dog and what is most beneficial for your breed. Experienced and conscientious breeders devote many years into developing a bloodline. In order to do this, he makes every effort to plan each breeding in regard to conformation,

A litter of eight has turned Spanish Ch. Laddland Fashionably Late into a "milk wagon." This picture was taken 45 days after whelping.

temperament and health. This type of breeder does his best to perform the necessary testing (i.e., OFA, CERF, testing for inherited blood disorders, thyroid, etc.). Testing is expensive and sometimes very disheartening when a favorite dog doesn't pass his health tests. The health history pertains not only to the breeding stock but to the immediate ancestors. Reputable breeders do not want their offspring to be bred indiscriminately. Therefore you may be asked to neuter or spay your puppy. Of course there is always the exception, and your breeder may agree to let you breed your dog under his direct supervision. This is an important concept. More and more effort is being made to breed healthier dogs.

Spay/Neuter

There are numerous benefits of performing this surgery at six months of age. Unspayed females are subject to mammary and ovarian cancer. In order to prevent mammary cancer she must be spayed prior to her first heat cycle. Later in life, an unspayed female may develop a pyometra (an infected uterus), which is definitely life threatening.

Spaying is performed under a general anesthetic and is easy on the young dog. As you might expect it is a little harder on the older dog, but that is no reason to deny her the surgery. The surgery removes the ovaries and uterus. It is important to remove all the ovarian tissue. If some is left behind, she could remain attractive to males. In order to view the ovaries, a reasonably long incision is necessary. An ovariohysterectomy is considered major surgery.

Neutering the male at a young age will inhibit some

Breeding should only be attempted by someone who is conscientious and knowledgeable. A litter of Sleepy Hollow pups owned by Bob and Ann Wlodkowsi play puppy games.

characteristic male behavior that owners frown upon. I have found my boys will not hike their legs and mark territory if they are neutered at six months of age. Also neutering at a young age has hormonal benefits, lessening the chance of hormonal aggressiveness.

Surgery involves removing the testicles but leaving the scrotum. If there should be a retained testicle, then he definitely needs to be neutered before the age of two or three years. Retained testicles can develop into cancer. Unneutered males are at risk for testicular cancer, perineal fistulas, perianal tumors and fistulas and prostatic disease.

Spaying/neutering is often the best option for your family pet. Your Dachshund will live a healthy and active life without the risk of certain cancers of the reproductive organs.

Intact males and females are prone to housebreaking accidents. Females urinate frequently before, during and after heat cycles, and males tend to mark territory if there is a female in heat. Males may show the same behavior if there is a visiting dog or guests.

Surgery involves a sterile operating procedure equivalent to human surgery. The incision site is shaved, surgically scrubbed and draped. The veterinarian wears a sterile surgical gown, cap, mask and gloves. Anesthesia should be monitored by a registered technician. It is customary for the veterinarian to recommend a pre-anesthetic blood screening, looking for metabolic problems and a ECG rhythm strip to check for normal heart function. Today anesthetics are equal to human anesthetics, which enables your dog to walk out of the clinic the same day as surgery.

Some folks worry about their dog gaining weight after being neutered or spayed. This is usually not the case. It is true that some dogs may be less active so they could develop a problem, but my own dogs are just as active as they were before surgery. I have a hard time keeping weight on them. However, if your dog should begin to gain, then you need to decrease his food and see to it that he gets a little more exercise.

DENTAL CARE for Your Dog's Life

S o you've got a new puppy! You also have a new set of puppy teeth in your household. Anyone who has ever raised a puppy is abundantly aware of these new teeth. Your puppy will chew anything it can reach, chase your shoelaces, and play "tear the rag" with any piece of clothing it can find. When puppies are newly born, they have no teeth. At about four weeks of age, puppies of most breeds begin to develop their deciduous or baby teeth. They begin eating semi-solid food, fighting and biting with their litter mates, and learning discipline from their mother. As their new teeth come in, they inflict more pain on their mother's breasts, so

"Tear the rag" is a favorite game for teething pups. A safe alternative is to provide your puppy with an array of quality chew products like the ones from Nylabone®.

This Nylafloss® is big enough for two miniature Dachshund pups to share. Nylafloss® is especially beneficial for puppies, as it aids in the removal of baby teeth.

her feeding sessions become less frequent and shorter. By six or eight weeks, the mother will start growling to warn her pups when they are fighting too roughly or hurting her as they nurse too much with their new teeth.

Puppies need to chew. It is a necessary part of their physical and mental development. They develop muscles and necessary life skills as they drag objects around, fight over possession, and vocalize alerts and warnings. Puppies chew on things to explore their world. They are using their sense of taste to determine what is food and what is not. How else can they tell an electrical cord from a lizard? At about four months of age, most puppies begin shedding their baby teeth. Often these teeth need some help to come out and make way for the permanent teeth. The incisors (front teeth) will be replaced first. Then, the adult canine or fang teeth erupt. When the baby tooth is not shed before the permanent tooth comes in, veterinarians call it a retained deciduous tooth. This condition will often cause gum infections by trapping hair and debris between the permanent tooth and the retained baby tooth. Nylafloss® is an excellent device for puppies to use. They can toss it, drag it, and chew on the many surfaces it presents. The baby teeth can catch in the nylon material, aiding in their removal. Puppies that have adequate chew toys will have less destructive behavior, develop more physically, and have less chance of retained deciduous teeth.

During the first year, your dog should be seen by your veterinarian at regular intervals. Your veterinarian will let you know when to bring in your puppy for vaccinations and parasite examinations. At each visit, your veterinarian should inspect the lips, teeth, and mouth as part of a complete physical examination. You should take some part in the maintenance of your dog's oral health. You should examine your dog's mouth weekly throughout his first year to make sure there are no sores, foreign objects, tooth problems, etc. If your dog drools excessively, shakes its head, or has bad breath, consult your veterinarian. By the time your dog is six months old, the permanent teeth are all in and plaque can start to accumulate on the tooth surfaces. This is when your dog needs to develop good dental-care habits to prevent calculus build-up on its teeth. Brushing is best. That is a fact that cannot be denied. However, some dogs do not like their teeth brushed regularly, or you may not be able to accomplish the task. In that case, you should consider a product that will help prevent plaque and calculus build-up.

The Plaque Attackers® and Galileo Bone® are other excellent choices for the first three years of a dog's life. Their shapes make them interesting for the dog. As the dog chews on them,

Teething puppies need to chew and they will sink their teeth into just about anything. Pups should be supervised to make sure they aren't getting into anything they shouldn't be.

the solid polyurethane massages the gums which improves the blood circulation to the periodontal tissues. Projections on the chew devices increase the surface and are in contact with the tooth for more efficient cleaning. The unique shape and consistency prevent your dog from exerting excessive force on his own teeth or from breaking off pieces of the bone. If your dog is an aggressive chewer or weighs more than 55 pounds (25 kg), you should consider giving him a Nylabone®, the most durable chew product on the market.

It is best to provide your Dachshund with a variety of chew toys so that he always has something to hold his interest (and keep him from gnawing on your new carpet!).

This Dachshund relaxes with his Plaque Attacker® bone. These durable chew toys have raised dental tips that massage the dog's gums and clean his teeth as he chews.

The Gumabone®, made by the Nylabone Company, is constructed of strong polyurethane, which is softer than nylon. Less powerful chewers prefer the Gumabones® to the Nylabones®. A super option for your dog is the Hercules Bone®, a uniquely shaped bone named after the great Olympian for its exceptional strength. Like all Nylabone products, they are specially scented to make them attractive to your dog. Ask your veterinarian about these bones and he will validate the good doctor's prescription: Nylabones® not only give your dog a good chewing workout but also help to save your dog's teeth (and even his life, as it protects him from possible fatal periodontal diseases).

By the time dogs are four years old, 75% of them have periodontal disease. It is the most common infection in dogs. Yearly examinations by your veterinarian are essential to maintaining your dog's good health. If your veterinarian detects periodontal disease, he or she may recommend a

That's a big Gumabone® for a miniature Dachshund! With Gumabone®'s wide variety, this little guy is sure to find something that's just his size.

Roar-Hide™ from Nylabone® is the safe alternative to rawhide. The rawhide is cut up, melted, and molded into a durable dog bone shape that won't break up and harm the dog.

prophylactic cleaning. To do a thorough cleaning, it will be necessary to put your dog under anesthesia. With modern gas anesthetics and monitoring equipment, the procedure is pretty safe. Your veterinarian will scale the teeth with an ultrasound scaler or hand instrument. This removes the calculus from the teeth. If there are calculus deposits below the gum line, the veterinarian will plane the roots to make them smooth. After all of the calculus has been removed, the teeth are polished with pumice in a polishing cup. If any medical or surgical treatment is needed, it is done at this time. The final step would be fluoride treatment and your follow-up treatment at home. If the periodontal disease is advanced, the veterinarian may prescribe a medicated mouth rinse or antibiotics for use at home. Make sure your dog has safe, clean and attractive chew toys and treats. Chooz® treats are another way of using a consumable treat to help keep your dog's teeth clean.

Rawhide is the most popular of all materials for a dog to chew. This has never been good news to dog owners, because rawhide is inherently very dangerous for dogs. Thousands of dogs have died from rawhide, having swallowed the hide after it has become soft and mushy, only to cause stomach and intestinal blockage. A new rawhide product on the market has finally solved the problem of rawhide: molded Roar-Hide® from Nylabone. These are composed of processed, cut up, and melted American rawhide injected into your dog's favorite shape: a dog bone. These dog-safe devices smell and taste like rawhide but don't break up. The ridges on the bones help to fight tartar build-up on the teeth and they last ten times longer than the usual rawhide chews.

You'll be rewarded with a lifetime of Dachshund kisses if you always make sure that your dog has the best dental care.

As your dog ages, professional examination and cleaning should become more frequent. The mouth should be inspected at least once a year. Your veterinarian may recommend visits every six months. In the geriatric patient, organs such as the heart, liver, and kidneys do not function as well as when they were young. Your veterinarian will probably want to test these organs' functions prior to using general anesthesia for dental cleaning. If your dog is a good chewer and you work closely with your veterinarian, your dog can keep all of its teeth all of its life. However, as your dog ages, his sense of smell, sight, and taste will diminish. He may not have the desire to chase, trap or chew his toys. He will also not have the energy to chew for long periods, as arthritis and periodontal disease make chewing painful. This will leave you with more responsibility for keeping his teeth clean and healthy. The dog that would not let you brush his teeth at one year of age, may let you brush his teeth now that he is ten years old.

If you train your dog with good chewing habits as a puppy, he will have healthier teeth throughout his life.

This miniature Smooth inspects his Gumaknot®. Gumabone® products by Nylabone® are good for puppies and less aggressive chewers due to their softer composition.

IDENTIFICATION and Finding the Lost Dog

There are several ways of identifying your dog. The old standby is a collar with dog license, rabies, and ID tags. Unfortunately collars have a way of being separated from the dog and tags fall off. I am not suggesting you shouldn't use a collar and tags. If they stay intact and on the dog, they are the quickest way of identification.

For several years owners have been tattooing their dogs. Some tattoos use a number with a registry. Here lies the problem because there are several registries to check. If you wish to tattoo, use your social security number. The humane shelters have the means to trace it. It is usually done on the inside of the rear thigh. The area is first shaved and numbed. There is no pain, although a few dogs do not like the buzzing sound.

The newest method of identification is microchipping. The microchip is a computer chip that is no bigger than a grain of rice.

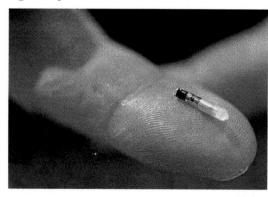

Occasionally tattooing is not legible and needs to be redone.

The newest method of identification is microchipping. The microchip is a computer chip that is no larger than a grain of rice. The veterinarian implants it by injection between the shoulder blades. The dog feels no discomfort. If your dog is lost and picked up by the humane society, they can trace you by scanning the microchip, which has its

The best way to find a lost dog is to prevent him from getting lost. Your dog should either be on a leash or under your watchful eye to keep him from going anywhere.

own code. Microchip scanners are friendly to other brands of microchips and their registries. The microchip comes with a dog tag saying the dog is microchipped. It is the safest way of identifying your dog.

FINDING THE LOST DOG

I am sure you will agree with me that there would be little worse than losing your dog. Responsible pet owners rarely lose their dogs. They do not let their dogs run free because they don't want harm to come to them. Not only that but in most, if not all, states there is a leash law.

Beware of fenced-in yards. They can be a hazard. Dogs find ways to escape either over or under the fence. Another fast exit is through the gate that perhaps the neighbor's child left unlocked.

Below is a list that hopefully will be of help to you if you need it. Remember don't give up, keep looking. Your dog is worth your efforts.

1. Contact your neighbors and put flyers with a photo on it in their mailboxes. Information you should include would be the dog's name, breed, sex, color, age, source of identification, when your dog was last seen and where, and your name and phone numbers. It may be helpful to say the dog needs medical care. Offer a *reward*.

Distributing flyers with your dog's picture and important information can be helpful in your search for the missing dog.

2. Check all local shelters daily. It is also possible for your dog to be picked up away from home and end up in an out-of-the-way shelter. Check these too. Go in person. It is not good enough to call. Most shelters are limited on the time they can hold dogs then they are put up for adoption or euthanized. There is the possibility that your dog will not make it to the shelter for several days. Your dog could have been wandering or someone may have tried to keep him.

3. Notify all local veterinarians. Call and send flyers.

4. Call your breeder. Frequently breeders are contacted when one of their breed is found.

5. Contact the rescue group for your breed.

6. Contact local schools—children may have seen your dog.

7. Post flyers at the schools, groceries, gas stations, convenience stores, veterinary clinics, groomers and any other place that will allow them.

8. Advertise in the newspaper.

9. Advertise on the radio.

A fenced-in yard and a locked gate are necessary if your Dachshund will be out in the yard. These are good safety measures but no guarantee that your dog will stay put.

TRAVELING with Your Dog

The earlier you start traveling with your new puppy or dog, the better. He needs to become accustomed to traveling. However, some dogs are nervous riders and become carsick easily. It is helpful if he starts with an empty stomach. Do not despair, as it will go better if you continue taking him with you on short fun rides. How would you feel if every time you rode in the car you stopped at the doctor's for an injection? You would soon dread that nasty car. Older dogs that tend to get carsick may have more of a problem adjusting to traveling. Those dogs that are having a serious problem may benefit from some medication prescribed by the veterinarian.

Do give your dog a chance to relieve himself before getting into the car. It is a good idea to be prepared for a clean up with a

Crates are a safe way for your dog to travel. The fiberglass crates are safest but the metal crates allow more air.

leash, paper towels, bag and terry cloth towel.

The safest place for your dog is in a fiberglass crate, although close confinement can promote carsickness in some dogs. If your dog is nervous you can try letting him ride on the seat next to you or in someone's lap.

An alternative to the crate would be to use a car harness made for dogs and/or a safety strap attached to the harness or collar. Whatever you do, do not let your dog ride in the back of a pickup truck unless he is securely tied on a very short lead. I've seen trucks stop quickly and, even though the dog was tied, it fell out and was dragged.

*"Don't forget about me!"
Once your Dachshund is
accustomed to traveling,
he may actually want to
come along for the ride.*

I do occasionally let my dogs ride loose with me because I really enjoy their companionship, but in all honesty they are safer in their crates. I have a friend whose van rolled in an accident but his dogs, in their fiberglass crates, were not injured nor did they escape. Another advantage of the crate is that it is a safe place to leave him if you need to run into the store. Otherwise you wouldn't be able to leave the windows down. Keep in mind that while many dogs are overly protective in their crates, this may not be enough to deter dognappers. In some states it is against the law to leave a dog in the car unattended.

Never leave a dog loose in the car wearing a collar and leash. I have known more than one dog that has killed himself by hanging. Do not let him put his head out an open window. Foreign debris can be blown into his eyes. When leaving your dog unattended in a car, consider the temperature. It can take less than five minutes to reach temperatures over 100 degrees Fahrenheit.

TRIPS

Perhaps you are taking a trip. Give consideration to what is best for your dog—traveling with you or boarding. When traveling by car, van or motor home, you need to think ahead about locking your vehicle. In all probability you have many valuables in the car and do not wish to leave it unlocked. Perhaps most valuable and not replaceable is your dog. Give thought to securing your vehicle and providing adequate ventilation for him. Another consideration for you when traveling with your dog is medical problems that may arise and little inconveniences, such as exposure to external parasites. Some areas of the country are quite flea infested. You may want to carry flea spray with you. This is even a good idea when staying in motels. Quite possibly you are not the only occupant of the room.

Unbelievably many motels and even hotels do allow canine guests, even some very first-class ones. Gaines Pet

These wirehaired Dachshunds know how to travel in style. Col. Katharine E. Manchester is a Dachshund owner who is proud to show her affection for her dogs.

Some Dachshunds prefer life in the fast lane. Ch. Luvadox Rose Parade poses on a Harley—the long seat is just her size!

Foods Corporation publishes *Touring With Towser*, a directory of domestic hotels and motels that accommodate guests with dogs. Their address is Gaines TWT, PO Box 5700, Kankakee, IL, 60902. I would recommend you call ahead to any motel that you may be considering and see if they accept pets. Sometimes it is necessary to pay a deposit against room damage. Of course you are more likely to gain accommodations for a small dog than a large dog. Also the management feels reassured when you mention that your dog will be crated. Since my dogs tend to bark when I leave the room, I leave the TV on nearly full blast to deaden the noises outside that tend to encourage my dogs to bark. If you do travel with your dog, take along plenty of baggies so that you can clean up after him. When we all do our share in cleaning up, we make it possible for motels to continue accepting our pets. As a matter of fact, you should practice cleaning up everywhere you take your dog.

Depending on where your are traveling, you may need an up-to-date health certificate issued by your veterinarian. It is good policy to take along your dog's medical information,

Dachshunds are easy to take along! Traveling with your dog doesn't have to be a hassle if you plan ahead and make the necessary arrangements.

which would include the name, address and phone number of your veterinarian, vaccination record, rabies certificate, and any medication he is taking.

AIR TRAVEL

When traveling by air, you need to contact the airlines to check their policy. Usually you have to make arrangements up to a couple of weeks in advance for traveling with your dog. The airlines require your dog to travel in an airline approved fiberglass crate. Usually these can be purchased through the airlines but they are also readily available in most pet-supply stores. If your dog is not accustomed to a crate, then it is a good idea to get him acclimated to it before your trip. The day of the actual trip you should withhold water about one hour ahead of departure and no food for about 12 hours. The airlines generally have temperature restrictions, which do not allow pets to travel if it is either too cold or too hot. Frequently these restrictions are based on the temperatures at the departure and arrival airports. It's best to inquire about a health certificate. These usually need to be issued within ten days of departure. You should arrange for non-stop, direct flights and if a commuter plane should be involved, check to see if it will carry dogs. Some don't. The Humane Society of the United States has put together a tip sheet for airline traveling. You can receive a copy by sending a self-addressed stamped envelope to:

The Humane Society of the United States
Tip Sheet
2100 L Street NW
Washington, DC 20037.

Exercise pens are portable and can be brought along on a trip to give your Dachshund a place to play once you reach your destination.

Regulations differ for traveling outside of the country and are sometimes changed without notice. Well in advance you need to write or call the appropriate consulate or agricultural department for instructions. Some countries have lengthy quarantines (six months), and countries differ in their rabies vaccination requirements. For instance, it may have to be given at least 30 days ahead of your departure.

Do make sure your dog is wearing proper identification. You never know when you might be in an accident and separated from your dog. Or your dog could be frightened and somehow manage to escape and run away. When I travel, my dogs wear collars with engraved nameplates with my name, phone number and city.

Another suggestion would be to carry in-case-of-emergency instructions. These would include the address and phone number of a relative or friend, your veterinarian's name, address and phone number, and your dog's medical information.

BOARDING KENNELS

Perhaps you have decided that you need to board your dog. Your veterinarian can recommend a good boarding facility or possibly a pet sitter that will come to your house. It is customary for the boarding kennel to ask for proof of vaccination for the DHLPP, rabies and bordetella vaccine. The bordetella should have been given within six months of boarding. This is for your protection. If they do not ask for this proof I would not board at their kennel.

Your family vacation wouldn't be complete without the whole family. A surprising number of destinations welcome dogs—check into it when planning your next trip.

For more information on pet sitting, contact NAPPS:

National Association of Professional Pet Sitters
1200 G Street, NW
Suite 760
Washington, DC 20005.

Our clinic has technicians that pet sit and technicians that board clinic patients in their homes. This may be an alternative for you. Ask your veterinarian if they have an employee that can help you. There is a definite advantage of having a technician care for your dog, especially if your dog is on medication or is a senior citizen.

You can write for a copy of *Traveling With Your Pet* from ASPCA, Education Department, 441 E. 92nd Street, New York, NY 10128.

A reputable boarding kennel will require that dogs receive the vaccination for kennel cough no less than two weeks before their scheduled stay.

BEHAVIOR and Canine Communication

Studies of the human/animal bond point out the importance of the unique relationships that exist between people and their pets. Those of us who share our lives with pets understand the special part they play through companionship, service and protection.

Senior citizens show more concern for their own eating habits when they have the responsibility of feeding a dog. Seeing that their dog is routinely exercised encourages the owner to think of schedules that otherwise may seem unimportant to the senior citizen. The older owner may be arthritic and feeling poorly but with responsibility for his dog he has a reason to get up and get moving. It is a big plus if his dog is an attention seeker who will demand such from his owner.

Dogs are a very important part of their owners' lives—the human/animal bond is a special one. Breeder Sandy Patterson and two of her Sandox puppies.

Over the last couple of decades, it has been shown that pets relieve the stress of those who lead busy lives. Owning a pet has been known to lessen the occurrence of heart attack and stroke.

Many single folks thrive on the companionship of a dog. Lifestyles are very different from a long time ago, and today more individuals seek the single life. However, they receive fulfillment from owning a dog.

Most likely the majority of our dogs live in family environments. The companionship they provide is well worth the effort involved. In my opinion, every child should have the opportunity to have a family dog. Dogs teach responsibility through understanding their care, feelings and even respecting their life cycles. Frequently those children who have not been exposed to dogs grow up afraid of dogs, which isn't good. Dogs sense timidity and some will take advantage of the situation.

Today more dogs are serving as service dogs. Since the origination of the Seeing Eye dogs years ago, we now have

Children make great playmates for energetic puppies. Most of all, caring for a puppy teaches a child responsibility and respect for animals.

trained hearing dogs. Also dogs are trained to provide service for the handicapped and are able to perform many different tasks for their owners. Search and Rescue dogs, with their handlers, are sent throughout the world to assist in recovery of disaster victims. They are life savers.

Therapy dogs are very popular with nursing homes, and some hospitals even allow them to visit. The inhabitants truly look forward to their visits. I have taken a couple of my dogs visiting and left in tears when I saw the response of the patients. They wanted and were allowed to have my dogs in their beds to hold and love.

Nationally there is a Pet Awareness Week to educate students and others about the value and basic care of our pets. Many countries take an even greater interest in their pets than Americans do. In those countries the pets are allowed to accompany their owners into restaurants and shops, etc. In the

U.S. this freedom is only available to our service dogs. Even so we think very highly of the human/animal bond.

CANINE BEHAVIOR

Canine behavior problems are the number-one reason for pet owners to dispose of their dogs, either through new homes, humane shelters or euthanasia. Unfortunately there are too many owners who are unwilling to devote the necessary time to properly train their dogs. On the other hand, there are those who not only are concerned about inherited health problems but are also aware of the dog's mental stability.

You may realize that a breed and his group relatives (i.e., sporting, hounds, etc.) show tendencies to behavioral characteristics. An experienced breeder can acquaint you with his breed's personality. Unfortunately many breeds are labeled with poor temperaments when actually the breed as a whole is not affected but only a small percentage of individuals within the breed.

Members of the same breed share the same background and, therefore, many of the same characteristics. However, every dog is an individual with a personality all his own.

If the breed in question is very popular, then of course there may be a higher number of unstable dogs. Do not label a breed good or bad. I know of absolutely awful-tempered dogs within one of our most popular, lovable breeds.

Inheritance and environment contribute to the dog's behavior. Some naïve people suggest inbreeding as the cause of bad temperaments. Inbreeding only results in poor behavior if the ancestors carry the trait. If there are excellent temperaments behind the dogs, then inbreeding will promote good temperaments in the offspring. Did you ever consider that inbreeding is what sets the characteristics of a breed? A purebred dog is the end result of inbreeding. This does not spare the mixed-breed dog from the same problems. Mixed-breed dogs frequently are the offspring of purebred dogs.

When planning a breeding, I like to observe the potential stud and his offspring in the show ring. If I see unruly behavior, I try to look into it further. I want to know if it is genetic or environmental, due to the lack of training and socialization. A good breeder will avoid breeding mentally unsound dogs.

Not too many decades ago most of our dogs led a different lifestyle than what is prevalent today. Usually mom stayed home so the dog had human companionship and someone to discipline it if needed. Not much was expected from the dog. Today's mom works and everyone's life is at a much faster pace.

Today's Dachshunds lead a very different lifestyle than that of their working ancestors. This Dachshund is ready to play after a hard day of lounging.

The dog may have to adjust to being a "weekend" dog. The family is gone all day during the week, and the dog is left to his own devices for entertainment. Some dogs sleep all day waiting for their family to come home and others become wigwam wreckers if given the opportunity. Crates do ensure the safety of the dog and the house. However, he could become physically and emotionally crippled if he doesn't get enough exercise and attention. We still appreciate and want the companionship of our dogs although we expect more from them. In many cases we tend to forget dogs are just that—*dogs* not human beings.

I own several dogs who are left crated during the day but I do try to make time for them in the evenings and on the weekends. Also we try to do something together before I leave

One of the most important aspects of a puppy's upbringing is socialization. A dog should grow up to be well-adjusted around people and animals, like Katie and her Sheltie friend.

for work. Maybe it helps them to have the companionship of other dogs. They accept their crates as their personal "houses" and seem to be content with their routine and thrive on trying their best to please me.

SOCIALIZING AND TRAINING

Many prospective puppy buyers lack experience regarding the proper socialization and training needed to develop the type of pet we all desire. In the first 18 months, training does take some work. Trust me, it is easier to start proper training before there is a problem that needs to be corrected.

The initial work begins with the breeder. The breeder should start socializing the puppy at five to six weeks of age and cannot let up. Human socializing is critical up through 12 weeks of age and likewise important during the following months. The litter should be left together during the first few weeks but it is necessary to separate them by ten weeks of age.

Leaving them together after that time will increase competition for litter dominance. If puppies are not socialized with people by 12 weeks of age, they will be timid in later life.

The eight- to ten-week age period is a fearful time for puppies. They need to be handled very gently around children and adults. There should be no harsh discipline during this time. Starting at 14 weeks of age, the puppy begins the juvenile period, which ends when he reaches sexual maturity around six to 14 months of age. During the juvenile period he needs to be introduced to strangers (adults, children and other dogs) on the home property. At sexual maturity he will begin to bark at strangers and become more protective. Males start to lift their legs to urinate but if you desire you can inhibit this behavior by walking your boy on leash away from trees, shrubs, fences, etc.

Perhaps you are thinking about an older puppy. You need to inquire about the puppy's social experience. If he has lived in a kennel, he may have a hard time adjusting to people and environmental stimuli. Assuming he has had a good social upbringing, there are advantages to an older puppy.

Training includes puppy kindergarten and a minimum of one to two basic training classes. During these classes you will learn how to dominate your youngster. This is especially important if you own a large breed of dog. It is somewhat harder, if not nearly impossible, for some owners to be the Alpha figure when their dog towers over them. You will be taught how to properly restrain your dog. This concept is important. Again it puts you in the Alpha position. All dogs need to be restrained many times during their lives. Believe it or not, some of our worst offenders are the eight-week-old puppies that are brought to our clinic. They need to be gently restrained for a nail trim but the way they carry on you would think we were killing them. In comparison, their vaccination is a "piece of cake." When we ask dogs to do something that is not agreeable to them, then their worst comes out. Life will be easier for your dog if you expose him at a young age to the necessities of life—proper behavior and restraint.

UNDERSTANDING THE DOG'S LANGUAGE

Most authorities agree that the dog is a descendent of the wolf. The dog and wolf have similar traits. For instance both are pack oriented and prefer not to be isolated for long periods of time. Another characteristic is that the dog, like the wolf, looks to the leader—Alpha—for direction. Both the wolf and the dog communicate through body language, not only within their pack but with outsiders.

Every pack has an Alpha figure. The dog looks to you, or should look to you, to be that leader. If your dog doesn't receive the proper training and guidance, he very well may replace you as Alpha. This would be a serious problem and is certainly a disservice to your dog.

Eye contact is one way the Alpha wolf keeps order within his pack. You are Alpha so you must establish eye contact with your puppy. Obviously your puppy will have to look at you. Practice eye contact even if you need to hold his head for five to ten seconds at a time. You can give him a treat as a reward. Make sure your eye contact is gentle and not threatening. Later, if he has been naughty, it is permissible to give him a long,

Let's hunt! Dogs often exhibit instinctive behavior—these adorable Longhair pups are on the prowl.

penetrating look. I caution you there are some older dogs that never learned eye contact as puppies and cannot accept eye contact. You should avoid eye contact with these dogs since they feel threatened and will retaliate as such.

Body Language

The play bow, when the forequarters are down and the hindquarters are elevated, is an invitation to play. Puppies play fight, which helps them learn the acceptable limits of biting. This is necessary for later in their lives. Nevertheless, an owner may be falsely reassured by the playful nature of his dog's aggression. Playful aggression toward another dog or human may be an indication of serious aggression in the future. Owners should never play fight or play tug-of-war with any dog that is inclined to be dominant.

Signs of submission are:

1. Avoids eye contact.
2. Active submission—the dog crouches down, ears back and the tail is lowered.
3. Passive submission—the dog rolls on his side with his hindlegs in the air and frequently urinates.

Signs of dominance are:

1. Makes eye contact.
2. Stands with ears up, tail up and the hair raised on his neck.
3. Shows dominance over another dog by standing at right angles over it.

Dominant dogs tend to behave in characteristic ways such as:

Dogs are so popular as pets because of their sociable nature. Two of Monica Canestrini's "children" (a human one and a wirehaired one) romp in the back yard.

1. The dog may be unwilling to move from his place (i.e., reluctant to give up the sofa if the owner wants to sit there).
2. He may not part with toys or objects in his mouth and may show possessiveness with his food bowl.
3. He may not respond quickly to commands.
4. He may be disagreeable for grooming and dislikes to be petted.

Who can resist these Dachshund faces? Five-month-old Legibach's Jewel Thief SS and future champion Legibach Treasured Jewel SS pose for the camera.

Dogs are popular because of their sociable nature. Those that have contact with humans during the first 12 weeks of life regard them as a member of their own species—their pack. All dogs have the potential for both dominant and submissive behavior. Only through experience and training do they learn to whom it is appropriate to show which behavior. Not all dogs are concerned with dominance but owners need to be aware of that potential. It is wise for the owner to establish his dominance early on.

A human can express dominance or submission toward a dog in the following ways:

1. Meeting the dog's gaze signals dominance. Averting the gaze signals submission. If the dog growls or threatens, averting the gaze is the first avoiding action to take—it may prevent attack. It is important to establish eye contact in the puppy. The older dog that has not been exposed to eye contact may see it as a threat and will not be willing to submit.
2. Being taller than the dog signals dominance; being lower signals submission. This is why, when attempting to make friends with a strange dog or catch the runaway, one should kneel down to his level. Some owners see their dogs become dominant when allowed on the furniture or on the bed. Then he is at the owner's level.

3. An owner can gain dominance by ignoring all the dog's social initiatives. The owner pays attention to the dog only when he obeys a command.

No dog should be allowed to achieve dominant status over any adult or child. Ways of preventing are as follows:

1. Handle the puppy gently, especially during the three- to four-month period.

2. Let the children and adults handfeed him and teach him to take food without lunging or grabbing.

3. Do not allow him to chase children or joggers.

4. Do not allow him to jump on people or mount their legs. Even females may be inclined to mount. It is not only a male habit.

5. Do not allow him to growl for any reason.

6. Don't participate in wrestling or tug-of-war games.

7. Don't physically punish puppies for aggressive behavior. Restrain him from repeating the infraction and teach an alternative behavior. Dogs should earn everything they receive from their owners. This

Ch. Candach's Hubbell, owned by Carl and Candace Holder, is pumped up and ready to show his dominance on the court.

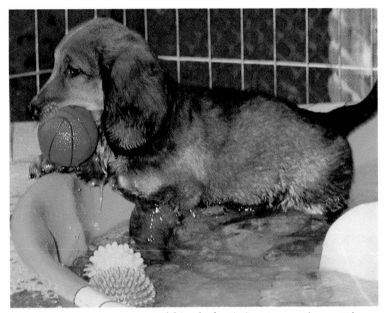

Ch. Ivic's Impulsive Gambler takes a dip in a baby pool— he's obviously not afraid of water!

would include sitting to receive petting or treats, sitting before going out the door and sitting to receive the collar and leash. These types of exercises reinforce the owner's dominance.

Young children should never be left alone with a dog. It is important that children learn some basic obedience commands so they have some control over the dog. They will gain the respect of their dog.

FEAR

One of the most common problems dogs experience is being fearful. Some dogs are more afraid than others. On the lesser side, which is sometimes humorous to watch, my dog can be afraid of a strange object. He acts silly when something is out of place in the house. I call his problem perceptive intelligence. He realizes the abnormal within his known environment. He does not react the same way in strange environments since he does not know what is normal.

On the more serious side is a fear of people. This can result in backing off, seeking his own space and saying "leave me alone" or it can result in an aggressive behavior that may lead

Dachshunds love "people food." These three Longhairs want a taste, but young Dan Wlodkowski doesn't look like he wants to share!

to challenging the person. Respect that the dog wants to be left alone and give him time to come forward. If you approach the cornered dog, he may resort to snapping. If you leave him alone, he may decide to come forward, which should be rewarded with a treat. Years ago we had a dog that behaved in this manner. We coaxed people to stop by the house and make friends with our fearful dog. She learned to take the treats and after weeks of work she overcame her suspicions and made friends more readily.

Some dogs may initially be too fearful to take treats. In these cases it is helpful to make sure the dog hasn't eaten for about 24 hours. Being a little hungry encourages him to accept the treats, especially if they are of the "gourmet" variety. I have a dog that worries about strangers since people seldom stop by my house. Over the years she has learned a cue and jumps up quickly to visit anyone sitting on the sofa. She learned by herself that all guests on the sofa were to be trusted friends. I think she felt more comfortable with them being at her level, rather than towering over her.

Dogs can be afraid of numerous things, including loud noises and thunderstorms. Invariably the owner rewards (by comforting) the dog when it shows signs of fearfulness. I had a terrible problem with my favorite dog in the Utility obedience class. Not only was he intimidated in the class but he was afraid of noise and afraid of displeasing me. Frequently he would knock down the bar jump, which clattered dreadfully. I gave him credit because he continued to try to clear it, although he was terribly scared. I finally learned to "reward" him every time he knocked down the jump. I would jump up and down, clap my hands and tell him how great he was. My psychology worked, he relaxed and eventually cleared the jump with ease. When your dog is frightened, direct his attention to something else and act happy. Don't dwell on his fright.

Ch. Grinzing's Magdalena W poses for a picture on the front steps.

AGGRESSION

Some different types of aggression are: predatory, defensive, dominance, possessive, protective, fear induced, noise provoked, "rage" syndrome (unprovoked aggression), maternal and aggression directed toward other dogs. Aggression is the most common behavioral problem encountered. Protective breeds are expected to be more aggressive than others but with the proper upbringing they can make very dependable companions. You need to be able to read your dog.

Many factors contribute to aggression including genetics and environment. An improper environment, which may include the living conditions, lack of social life, excessive punishment, being attacked or frightened by an aggressive dog, etc., can all influence a dog's behavior. Even spoiling him and giving too much praise may be detrimental.
Isolation and the lack of human contact or exposure to frequent teasing by children or adults also can ruin a good dog.

From ten-week-old puppy to champion...future Best in Show winner Ch. Jeric's Delightfully Dana W (bottom) and a littermate.

Lack of direction, fear, or confusion lead to aggression in those dogs that are so inclined. Any obedience exercise, even the sit and down, can direct the dog and overcome fear and/or confusion. Every dog should learn these commands as a youngster, and there should be periodic reinforcement.

When a dog is showing signs of aggression, you should speak calmly (no screaming or hysterics) and firmly give a command that he understands, such as the sit. As soon as your dog obeys, you have assumed your dominant position. Aggression presents a problem because there may be danger to others. Sometimes it is an emotional issue. Owners may consciously or unconsciously encourage their dog's aggression. Other owners show responsibility by accepting the problem and taking measures to keep it under control. The owner is responsible for his dog's actions, and it is not wise to take a chance on someone being bitten, especially a child. Euthanasia is the solution for some owners and in severe cases this may be the best choice. However, few dogs are that dangerous and very few are that much of a threat to their owners. If caution is exercised and professional help is gained

Dachshunds, like most dogs, are naturally inquisitive and love to explore. This Smooth sniffs around in search of something interesting.

early on, then I surmise most cases can be controlled.

Some authorities recommend feeding a lower protein (less than 20 percent) diet. They believe this can aid in reducing aggression. If the dog loses weight, then vegetable oil can be added. Veterinarians and behaviorists are having some success with pharmacology. In many cases treatment is possible and can improve the situation.

If you have done everything according to "the book" regarding training and socializing and are still having a behavior problem, don't procrastinate. It is important that the problem gets attention before it is out of hand. It is estimated that 20 percent of a veterinarian's time may be devoted to dealing with problems before they become so intolerable that the dog is separated from its home and owner. If your veterinarian isn't able to help, he should refer you to a behaviorist.

When your Dachshund flashes those "puppy dog" eyes, you might just let him get away with anything! Remember—you are the dominant one, not the puppy.

PROBLEMS

Barking

This is a habit that shouldn't be encouraged. Over the years I've had new puppy owners call to say that their dog hasn't learned to bark. I assure them they are indeed fortunate but not to worry. Some owners desire their dog to bark so as to be a watchdog. In my experience, most dogs will bark when a stranger comes to the door.

The new puppy frequently barks or whines in the crate in his strange environment and the owner reinforces the puppy's bad behavior by going to him during the night. This is a no-no. I tell my new owners to smack the top of the crate and say "quiet" in a loud, firm voice. The puppies don't like to hear the loud noise of the crate being banged. If the barking is sleep-interrupting, then the owner should take crate and pup to the bedroom for a few days until the

Elsa loves the attention she gets from her young friend. Photo courtesy of Model Team, Ocean Grove, NJ.

puppy becomes adjusted to his new environment. Otherwise ignore the barking during the night.

Barking can be an inherited problem or a bad habit learned through the environment. It takes dedication to stop the barking. Attention should be paid to the cause of the barking. Does the dog seek attention, does he need to go out, is it feeding time, is it occurring when he is left alone, is it a protective bark, etc.? Presently I have a ten-week-old puppy that is a real loud mouth, which I am sure is an inherited tendency. Both her mother and especially her grandmother are overzealous barkers but fortunately have mellowed with the years. My young puppy is corrected with a firm "no" and gentle shaking and she is responding. When barking presents a problem for you, try to stop it as soon as it begins.

There are electronic collars available that are supposed to curb barking. Personally I have not had experience with them. There are some disadvantages to to the collar. If the dog is barking out of excitement, punishment is not the appropriate treatment. Presumably there is the chance the collar could be activated by other stimuli and thereby punish the dog when it is not barking. Should you decide to use one, then you should seek help from a person with experience with that type of collar. In my opinion I feel the root of the problem needs to be investigated and corrected.

In extreme circumstances (usually when there is a problem with the neighbors), some people have resorted to having their dogs debarked. I caution you that the dog continues to bark but usually only a squeaking sound is heard. Frequently the vocal cords grow back. Probably the biggest concern is that the dog can be left with scar tissue which can narrow the opening to the trachea.

Jumping Up

Personally, I am not thrilled when other dogs jump on me

Dogs have many different ways of showing affection. Elsa loves her owner, John Merriman.

This group of wirehaired Dachshunds has the potential to make a lot of noise!

but I have hurt feelings if they don't! I do encourage my own dogs to jump on me, on command. Some do and some don't. In my opinion, a dog that jumps up is a happy dog. Nevertheless few guests appreciate dogs jumping on them. Clothes get footprinted and/or snagged.

I am a believer in allowing the puppy to jump up during his first few weeks. In my opinion if you correct him too soon and at the wrong age you may intimidate him. Consequently he could be timid around humans later in his life. However, there will come a time, probably around four months of age, that he needs to know when it is okay to jump and when he is to show off good manners by sitting instead.

Some authorities never allow jumping. If you are irritated by your dog jumping up on you, then you should discourage it from the beginning. A larger breed of dog can cause harm to a senior citizen. Some are quite fragile. It may not take much to cause a topple that could break a hip.

How do you correct the problem? All family members need

to participate in teaching the puppy to sit as soon as he starts to jump up. The sit must be practiced every time he starts to jump up. Don't forget to praise him for his good behavior. If an older dog has acquired the habit, grasp his paws and squeeze tightly. Give a firm "No." He'll soon catch on. Remember the entire family must take part. Each time you allow him to jump up you go back a step in training.

Biting

All puppies bite and try to chew on your fingers, toes, arms, etc. This is the time to teach them to be gentle

*Eggs, vegetables, hot dogs... **hot dogs**?? How did these Dachshund puppies get mixed in with the groceries?*

and not bite hard. Put your fingers in your puppy's mouth and if he bites too hard then say "easy" and let him know he's hurting you. I squeal and act like I have been seriously hurt. If the puppy plays too rough and doesn't respond to your corrections, then he needs "Time Out" in his crate. You should be particularly careful with young children and puppies who still have their deciduous (baby) teeth. Those teeth are like needles and can leave little scars on youngsters.

Biting in the more mature dog is something that should be prevented at all costs. Should it occur I would quickly let him know in no uncertain terms that biting will not be tolerated. When biting is directed toward another dog (dog fight), don't get in the middle of it. On more than one occasion I have had to separate a couple of my dogs and usually was in the middle of that one last lunge by the offender. Some authorities recommend breaking up a fight by elevating the hind legs. This would only be possible if there was a person for each dog. Obviously it would be hard to fight with the hind legs off the ground. A dog bite is serious and should be given attention. Wash the bite with soap and water and contact your doctor. It is important to know the status of the offender's rabies vaccination.

I have several dogs that are sensitive to having mats combed out of their coats and eventually they have had enough. They give fair warning by turning and acting like they would like to nip my offending fingers. However, one verbal warning from me says, "I'm sorry, don't you dare think about biting me and please let me carefully comb just a little bit more." I have owned a minimum of 30 dogs and raised many more puppies

Sure, dogs like to chew...and it looks like some dog owners do, too! Baron shares a toy with his owner Ed Docke.

and have yet to have one of my dogs bite me except during that last lunge in the two or three dog fights I felt compelled to break up. My dogs wouldn't dare bite me. They know who is boss.

This is not always the case for other owners. I do not wish to frighten you but when biting occurs you should seek professional help at once. On the other hand you must not let your dog intimidate you and be so afraid of a bite that you can't discipline him. Professional help through your veterinarian, dog trainer and/or behaviorist can give you guidance.

Digging

Bored dogs release their frustrations through mischievous behavior such as digging. For the life of me I do not understand why people own dogs only to keep them outside. Dogs shouldn't be left unattended outside, even if they are in a fenced-in yard. Usually the dog is sent to "jail" (the backyard) because the owner can't tolerate him in the house. The culprit feels socially deprived and needs to be included in the owner's life. The owner has neglected the dog's training. The dog has not developed into the companion we desire. If you are one of these owners, then perhaps it is possible for you to change. Give him another chance. Some owners object to their dog's unkempt coat and doggy odor. See that he is groomed on a regular schedule and look into some training classes.

Submissive Urination

This is not a housebreaking problem. It can occur in all breeds and may be more prevalent in some breeds. Usually it occurs in puppies but occasionally it occurs in older dogs and may be in response to physical praise. Try verbal praise or ignoring your dog until after he has had a chance to relieve himself. Scolding will only make the problem worse. Many dogs outgrow this problem.

Many behavior problems are common in puppies, but just like children, they will hopefully outgrow these behaviors as they mature.

Coprophagia

Also know as stool eating, sometimes occurs without a cause. It may begin with boredom and then becomes a habit that is hard to break. Your best remedy is to keep the puppy on a leash and keep the yard picked up. Then he won't have an opportunity to get in trouble. I do not like to clean up accidents or "poop scoop" the yard in front of puppies. I'm suspicious that some puppies try to help and will clean up the stool before I have a chance. Your veterinarian can dispense a medication that is put on the dog's food that makes the stool taste bitter. Of course this will do little good if your dog cleans up after other dogs.

The Runaway

There is little excuse for a dog to run away since dogs should never be off leash except when supervised in the fenced-in yard.

I receive phone calls on a regular basis from prospective owners that want to purchase a female since a male is inclined to roam. It is true that an intact male is inclined to roam, which is one of the reasons a male should be neutered. However, females will roam also, especially if they are in heat. Regardless, these dogs should never be given this opportunity. A few years ago one of our clients elected euthanasia for her elderly dog that radiographically appeared to have an intestinal blockage. The veterinarian suggested it might be a corncob. She assured him that was not possible since they hadn't had any. Apparently he roamed and raided the neighbor's garbage and you guessed it—he had a corncob blocking his intestines. Another dog raided the neighbor's garbage and died from toxins from the garbage.

Dachshunds are known for their personality, and each dog is unique. This Smooth is one of the more intellectual types.

To give the benefit of the doubt, perhaps your dog escapes or perhaps you are playing with your dog in the yard and he refuses to come when called. You now have a runaway. I have had this happen on a smaller scale in the house and have, even to my embarrassment, witnessed this in the obedience ring. Help! The first thing to remember is when you finally do catch your naughty dog, you must not discipline him. The reasoning behind this is that it is quite possible there could be a repeat performance, and it would be nice if the next time he would respond to your sweet command.

Four-week-old puppies pose as part of this "still life"—an amazing feat considering how hard it is for puppies to keep still!

Always kneel down when trying to catch the runaway. Dogs are afraid of people standing over them. Also it would be helpful to have a treat or a favorite toy to help entice him to your side. After that initial runaway experience, start practicing the recall with your dog. You can let him drag a long line (clothesline) and randomly call him and then reel him in. Let him touch you first. Reaching for the dog can frighten him. Each time he comes you reward him with a treat and eventually he should get the idea that this is a nice experience. The long line prevents him from really getting out of hand. My dogs tend to come promptly within about 3 to 4 feet (out of reach) and then turn tail and run. It's "catch me if you can." At least with the long line you can step on it and stop him.

Food Guarding

If you see signs of your puppy guarding his food, then you should take immediate steps to correct the problem. It is not fair to your puppy to feed him in a busy environment where children or other pets may interfere with his eating. This can be the cause of food guarding. I always recommend that my puppies be fed in their crates where they do not feel threatened. Another advantage of this is that the puppy gets down to the business of eating and doesn't fool around. Perhaps you have seen possessiveness over the food bowl or his toys. Start by feeding him out of your hand and teach him that it is okay for you to remove his food bowl or toy and that you most assuredly will return it to him. If your dog is truly a bad actor and intimidates you, try keeping him on leash and perhaps sit next to him making happy talk. At feeding time make him work for his reward (his dinner) by doing some obedience command such as sit or down. Before your problem gets out of control you should get professional help. If he is out of control over toys, perhaps you should dispose of them or at least put them away when young children are around.

Mischief and Misbehavior

All puppies and even some adult dogs will get into mischief at some time in their lives. You should start by "puppy proofing" your house. Even so it is impossible to have a sterile environment. For instance, if you would be down to four walls and a floor your dog could still chew a hole in the wall. What do you do? Remember puppies should never be left unsupervised so let us go on to the trusted adult dog that has misbehaved. His behavior may be an attention getter. Dogs, and even children, are known to do mischief even though they know they will be punished. Your puppy/dog will benefit from

The innocent faces of three cute Dachshund pups. Dachshund puppies are adorable in any color.

more attention and new direction. He may benefit from a training class or by reinforcing the obedience he has already learned. How about a daily walk? That could be a good outlet for your dog, time together and exercise for both of you.

This Longhair pup enjoys hanging out with someone his own age. He surprises his young friend with a big kiss.

Separation Anxiety

This occurs when dogs feel distress or apprehension when separated from their owners. One of the mistakes owners make is to set their dogs up for their departure. Some authorities recommend paying little attention to the pet for at least ten minutes before leaving and for the first ten minutes after you arrive home. The dog isn't cued to the fact you are leaving and if you keep it lowkey they learn to accept it as a normal everyday occurrence. Those dogs that are used to being crated usually accept your departure. Dogs that are anxious may have a serious problem and wreak havoc on the house within a few minutes after your departure. You can try to acclimate your dog to the separation by leaving for just a few minutes at a time, returning and rewarding him with a treat. Don't get too carried away. Plan on this process taking a long time. A behaviorist can set down a schedule for you. Those dogs that are insecure, such as ones obtained from a humane shelter or those that have changed homes, present more of a problem.

Punishment

A puppy should learn that correction is sometimes necessary and should not question your authority. An older dog that has never received correction may retaliate. In my opinion there will be a time for physical punishment but this does not mean hitting the dog. Do not use newspapers, fly swatters, etc. One type of correction, that is used by the mother dog when she corrects her puppies, is to take the puppy by the scruff and shake him *gently*. For the older, larger dog you can grab the scruff, one hand on each side of his neck, and lift his legs off the ground. This is effective since dogs feel intimidated when their feet are off the ground. Timing is of the utmost importance when punishment is necessary. Depending on the degree of fault, you might want to reinforce punishment by ignoring your dog for 15 to 20 minutes. Whatever you do, do not overdo corrections or they will lose value.

My most important advice to you is to be aware of your dog's actions. Even so, remember dogs are dogs and will behave as such even though we might like them to be perfect little people. You and your dog will become neurotic if you worry about every little indiscretion. When there is reason for concern—don't waste time. Seek guidance. Dogs are meant to be loved and enjoyed.

References:

Manual of Canine Behavior, Valerie O'Farrell, British Small Animal Veterinary Association.

Good Owners, Great Dogs, Brian Kilcommons, Warner Books.

Laid back, relaxed...this is the life! Although not all Dachshunds can swim, many take a liking to the water. Lacey floats the day away in the family pool.

SUGGESTED READING

PS-822
The Dachshund
320 pages,
190 full-color
photos.

TS-258
Training your Dog for
Sports and Other Activities
160 pages, over 200 full-
color photos.

TS-249
Skin & Coat Care for
your Dog
224 pages, over 190
full-color photos.

TS-214
Owner's Guide to Dog
Health
432 pages, over 300 full-
color photos.

INDEX